TO HOLLAND AND TO NEW HARMONY

Robert Dale Owen's Travel Journal

1825-1826

Edited by Josephine M. Elliott

INDIANA HISTORICAL SOCIETY · INDIANAPOLIS · 1969

COPYRIGHT © 1969
BY THE
INDIANA HISTORICAL SOCIETY

Printed in the United States
of America

INDIANA

HISTORICAL SOCIETY

PUBLICATIONS

VOLUME 23

NUMBER 4

Courtesy of Kenneth Dale Owen

Robert Dale Owen at Age Nineteen
by David Dale Owen

INTRODUCTION

Like many of his contemporaries, Robert Dale Owen kept journals of his daily activities, his thoughts and ideas; like some, he used these numerous journals for later publications. While the articles and books drawn from these journals have the added advantage of a more graceful and considered style and a leisurely pace, the accounts of on-the-spot happenings, reactions only hours later, contain the fresh quality of initial impressions, and—in some instances—a more accurate account of the actual event.

Oldest son of Robert Owen, the philanthropist and pioneer in the co-operative movement, and Anne Caroline Dale Owen, Robert Dale Owen was born November 7, 1801, in Glasgow. His childhood was spent at Braxfield, the Owen family home outside New Lanark where his father's cotton mills were located. Between the ages of seventeen and twenty-one he attended a school, along with his brother William, at Hofwyl, near Bern, Switzerland, maintained by Philipp Emanuel von Fellenberg, a follower of the Pestalozzian system of education. After his return to Scotland he became a teacher and superintendent in the progressive New Lanark schools established by his father.

Robert Owen sailed for America on October 23, 1824, to negotiate the purchase of Harmonie (New Harmony) as the site for his experiment in communal living. The property, located on the Wabash River in Posey County, southwestern Indiana, included the thriving village built by the Harmonists, or Rappites, a sectarian society of Würtemberg peasants, so-called after the founder George Rapp, and twenty thousand acres of land. Owen arrived back in England on August 6,

175

1825. Though Robert Dale had been eager to participate in this transaction, the father took with him instead the younger William, leaving Robert Dale in charge of the New Lanark mills.

The period chronicled in the present journal begins on May 30, 1825, during the father's absence, and extends to January 23, 1826, the day Robert Dale arrived in New Harmony, having accompanied his father on the latter's second journey to America. During June 1825, Robert Dale traveled to Holland where he took an extended trip in company with an old schoolmate to study the Dutch co-operative communities. The minuteness of his observation and detailed reporting of the "colonies" at Fredericks-Oord, Veenhuisen, and Omerschanz, attest to the deep interest he felt in and knowledge he possessed of the co-operative movements of his time.

Highlight of July was a brief tour of some historic and scenic places in Scotland in the company of his mother, three sisters—Anne, Mary, and Jane—and Margaret,[1] the attractive young girl whom he loved and hoped eventually to marry.

In August, with Robert Owen's arrival home, preparations for his return to America, this time accompanied by Robert Dale, took precedence over other activities; and on September 27, Robert Dale left Braxfield for the long ocean voyage which terminated at New York on November 6, the eve of his twenty-fourth birthday. Approximately a month was spent in and around New York and Philadelphia. So enthusiastic was Robert Dale's response to the New World that within a week of his arrival he went to a public court and declared his intention of becoming an American citizen.

The final leg of the trip for Robert Dale, also by water, began on December 8, at Pittsburgh, where the Owen party purchased a keelboat, the "Philanthropist," and ended with the the arrival of this famous "Boatload of Knowledge" at Mount Vernon, Indiana, January 23, 1826. One month of the intervening time, however, was spent near Beaver, Pennsylvania, at

To Holland and To New Harmony

a "station" called Safe Harbor, where the keelboat was grounded in the ice. This period, while onerous for some of the party, was a thoroughly delightful one for Robert Dale, who employed himself almost daily in hunting and absorbing woods lore in the daytime and reading the French social reformer Fourier at night. In one of his German asides he says, "The ladies are becoming evermore disgusted, particularly S.T. [Sarah Turner] who cried this morning during breakfast. It is somewhat of a good education for her and for all of us. As for myself, seldom have I had a better time."

From Mount Vernon the impatient young Robert Dale set out immediately on horseback for New Harmony and "arrived just in time to hear my father address the inhabitants."

Though unpublished in its entirety up to the present, this journal was used by Robert Dale as a primary source for a series of articles in *The New-Harmony Gazette* entitled "The Dutch and Their Country."[2] For these he lifted practically intact pages of his description of the co-operative labor colonies in Holland, omitting only observations of a personal or possibly "offensive" nature, and making some alterations for publication purposes. The most fascinating portion of the journal for those interested in New Harmony history—the journey of the "Philanthropist" down the Ohio River with its precious cargo of intellectuals—Robert Dale seems not to have utilized in his later writings except in a general way. Forty-eight years later, in his autobiography, *Threading My Way*, his memory is somewhat dimmed as to the party's makeup, and he includes among the passengers persons not on the boat and omits some who, according to this firsthand account, were.[3]

Also excluded from any of the published writings are the charming asides in German which impart a quality of immediacy to the scene, and offer insights into the personalities of both observer and observed. For example, Mme Fretageot is revealed as a strong, intelligent woman whom Robert Dale admires for her adaptability and good sense, and to whom he turns as a confidante. Could it be that his long conversations about his "situation at home" were concerned with his love for the young Margaret left behind? William Maclure seems to Robert Dale to be hard to get along with, stubborn, suspicious, and quarrelsome. Donald Macdonald, too, does not appear to fit Robert Dale's idea of what a communitarian should be. Nor does Robert Owen *père* fare too well, either. His son thinks him too dogmatic and his manner of presenting his ideas too vehement: "He tends to fall into the same fault which he criticizes in others."

Robert Dale reveals himself as a young enthusiast who is fascinated by the American backwoods life and people; perceptive and highly intelligent; strongly optimistic and sanguine about "community life." Was this young cosmopolite also so delicate and ingenuous—or secretive—that he could speak of "the ladies" only in German, even when it was merely to report that they "are somewhat better"?

The remark of Richard W. Leopold, biographer of Robert Dale Owen, "The curious will find the pages [of *Threading My Way*] delightful reading, but they tell more of Owen the septuagenarian than of Owen the child"[4] characterizes the differences between this journal and the later writings.

Four persons wrote accounts of the group of individuals who joined Robert Owen and William Maclure in their New Harmony venture and journeyed on the "Philanthropist": Charles Alexandre Lesueur, Donald Macdonald (who boarded the keelboat January 7, 1826), Victor Duclos (then a child of six), and Robert Dale Owen. The first two kept notebooks during the trip down the river; Duclos' *Recollections* and Robert Dale's *Atlantic* articles and autobiography were written years later. Now, with the availability of this journal, also kept during the journey, new light is shed upon hitherto unresolved questions regarding the passenger list.[5]

To Holland and To New Harmony

After the collapse of the New Harmony community Robert Dale Owen remained in America, serving both the State of Indiana and the nation as legislator, congressman, and diplomat in the 1840's and 1850's. The final twenty years of his life were devoted to writing, lecturing, and espousing spiritualism. He died in 1877.[6]

The text of the present journal, including the German passages, is reproduced here as written, complete with errors and abbreviations. However, what are obviously mere slips of the pen have been corrected and words unintentionally repeated have been omitted. The word "and" has been used instead of the ampersand consistently employed by Robert Dale.

The original journal is in the Roger D. Branigin–Kenneth Dale Owen Collection of the New Harmony Workingmen's Institute Library, purchased in October 1967 from Eleanor Stone Perenyi, a descendant of Robert Dale Owen. Grateful acknowledgment is made to the donors of the collection, Governor Branigin, long-time friend and staunch supporter of New Harmony, and Kenneth Dale Owen, great-great-grandson of Robert Owen, who granted permission to publish the journal. The collection up to the time of purchase had been in the possession of the Robert Dale Owen branch of the Owen family and has been cited by researchers who were permitted access to it as the Julian Dale Owen Papers and/or the Grace Zaring Stone Manuscripts.

Three other people deserve special thanks for their help: Miss Gayle Thornbrough, director of Publications of the Indiana Historical Society, for suggestions and direction; Dr. Alfred Niedermayer for the German translations; and Mrs. Jo Ann Medcalf, who carefully and painstakingly typed the manuscript.

The originals of the drawing of Robert Dale Owen by his brother David Dale and the water color of Braxfield, thought to have been painted by either Robert Dale or David Dale, are the property of Kenneth Dale Owen and permission to reproduce them is gratefully acknowledged. The originals of the drawings by Charles Alexandre Lesueur are in the possession of the Muséum d'Histoire Naturelle, Le Harve. Prints for inclusion herein were obtained from reproductions in the American Philosophical Society Library, Philadelphia. The drawings of Fredericks-Oord and Veenhuisen are reproduced from *An Account of the Poor-Colonies and Agricultural Workhouses of the Benevolent Society of Holland* (Edinburgh, 1828).

The Indiana Historical Society has issued in its *Publications* series William Owen's diary of his journey to New Harmony with his father, 1824–1825, the diaries of Donald Macdonald of his two journeys to New Harmony, 1824–1826, the papers of Thomas and Sarah Pears, members of the New Harmony community, and selections of the correspondence of Mme Fretageot and William Maclure. It is fitting that this travel journal of Robert Dale Owen should appear in this series.

J. M. E.

TO HOLLAND AND TO NEW HARMONY

Monday May 30th 1825.

Left Braxfield[1] for Edinburgh, accompanied by Higgins;[2] arrived abt 3, and executed various commissions.

Tuesday May 31st.

Executed various commissions in Edinb. Dined at William Campbell's with A. Combe[3] and Dr. Yule.

Wednesday June 1.

Set sail in the Soho, steam packet for London. Side wind and variable weather.

Thursday June 2 &
Friday June 3.

Wind a-head and weather changeable. Arrived on Friday night or rather Saturday morng early at Blackwall. The voyage was, on the whole extremely pleasant; not at all tedious and all ended with no fatigue. I prefer this to any other mode of travelling.

Saturday June 4.

Breakfasted at Plough Court,[4] where I heard that the Infant School Meeting[5] was to be held that day. Took lodgings at 34 Southampton St. Strand, and then proceeded to the meeting, where I found almost all our London friends, John Smith,[6] Morrison,[7] Hart, Morgan,[8] Skene[9] — Day wet, but the meeting well attended, especially by ladies. Much tedious longwinded speaking, little to the point. Irving[10] was tiresome and I think illiberal, but, I believe, with the best intentions.

Courtesy of Kenneth Dale Owen

Braxfield, Robert Owen's Home at New Lanark

*Water color attributed to either
Robert Dale Owen or David Dale Owen*

Brougham[11] spoke in a shuffling manner and his speech went for nothing. The feeling of the meeting, as evinced by applause, was decidedly in favor of liberality and freedom and against fanaticism and illiberality. Not one individual, however, ventures to speak his real sentiments, particularly on the subject of religion; nor was it even suggested that this abstruse science might be too difficult for the comprehension of infants. I fear the meeting was not likely materially to promote the interests of the society. I dined with Higgins, Philipp Chapeaurouge and Völker, whose gymnastics succeed pretty well. Went to the theatre to hear the Freischütz.[12] The music is original, beautiful and most expressive, the tale most unnatural and the scenery most horrible and terrific.

To Holland and To New Harmony

Sunday June 5.

Breakfasted with John Smith, and had afterwards a long conversation with him and his lady. They are most ameable, kind people, but I fear so circumstanced, that they can do but little good; and that they are neither satisfied nor happy in their present circle. Called on Morgan and on Silvester—neither at home. Dined at 10 Artillery Place with Mr. Lepard,[13] where I met Cowper,[14] Morgan, Skene, Thompson,[15] Miss Cowper, Miss Applegath, etc. Thompson was violent and I think injudicious in his conversation; he particularly undervalues the value of gymnastic exercises.

Monday June 6.

Skene breakfasted with us and we went with him to the Cooperative Society,[16] 18 Pukett St. where there were several good rooms. Took a Dutch lesson. Called with Skene on Mrs. Kemmis who appears to be a most superior woman. In the evening went with Morgan to the Christian evidence Society—a moral phenomenon. Taylor, the leader, was amusing and witty, employed no sound arguments against the advocates of Christianity, his opponents, but merely ridicule and satire, veiled under the thinnest veil of mock conformity, that wd shelter him from the law against blasphemy. I am sure he convinced no one; and I believe that he amused the greater part of his audience and offended the rest. I cannot say that I in any way approve of the spirit in which the discussion was conducted. Properly conducted it might I conceive do infinite good.

Tuesday June 7.

Wrote a paragraph for the Times regardg Völkers gymnastics. Called abt our passports. Called on Mr. Phillips. R. A.[17] Dined with Mr. Hart after calling on Mrs. Stewart.[18] Met at Mr. Hart's a Mr. Wagner, a pleasant Canadian gentleman. He says he thinks we will be pleased with America, and that the greatest inconvenience we experience will be from the excessive heat of the summer.

Wednesday June 8.

After breakfast visited Somerset house.[19] Collection good, particularly Sir Thos Lawrence's portrait of young Lambton,[20] where the figure appeared actually to start from the canvass. Visited Völkers gymnastic school, where I met Cowper, Leigh Hunt,[21] and several other young men, who appear to take up the matter most warmly and in the proper spirit. Had a conversation with Völker, in which he stated to me that he had got into considerable difficulties, and I promised what I could to assist him out of them.

Thursday June 9.

Breakfasted with Mrs. Stewart. Called on Richmond. I received no very favorable impression of him from this visit. His habits appear slovenly and I incline to think him intriguing; but I may be mistaken. Called on Joseph Foster[22] and Michael Gibbs,[23] but found both out of town. Delivered Margaret's[24] letter to her grandmother, 10 Barking Church Yard, who seems an excellent sort of person; and who highly approved of Margaret's going with us to America. Took our places in Steamboat. Dined with C. Hanbury[25] at Plough Court, where I met young Joseph Foster. Went out to Stoke-Newington and found W. Allen[26] most intent upon his plans for schools and cottages—very friendly—but I think in low spirits. Gray[27] drank tea with us and we went to the Cooperative Society. The attendance of members small and but little spirit evinced among them. I spoke in reply to a young man who made some remarks on my fathers discourse.

Friday June 10.

Went with Skene to breakfast with a young lady of the name of Hamilton, who appears sensible and pleasant. Called abt our passports etc. Called on Barnes the editor of the Times,[28] to ask him to insert my fathers discourses[29] and a paragraph regarding gymnastics; but I doubt if he will attend to either. Called at 49 Bedford Sqr,[30] but found them out. Called at Silvesters to ask for Whitwell,[31] but he is not in town. Dined with Higgins and Philipp.

Saturday June 11.

Set out in the "King of the Netherlands" Steamboat for Rotterdam; but we had not proceeded far above ten minutes when part of the engine gave way and we were at first afraid that we should be obliged to proceed with one engine only; but after a detension of about five hours, we had it repaired and proceeded. The day was beautiful, but exceedingly hot, till we got fairly out to sea.

Sunday June 12.

Day fine, and warm. Came in sight of Holland about 2 o'clock. A quantity of porpoises followed the ship for a considerable time, playing round at the distance, sometimes, of a few yards only. The coast is exceedingly low, and the passage into the Meuse narrow and difficult of navigation. We saw several wrecks on a sandbank near to us. The land seems well wooded; and the villages as we sailed up the Meuse appeared to great advantage on the banks, generally situated on canals: the inhabitants, it being Sunday, were assembled in many places in crowds in their best attire, apparently for the purpose of seeing the boat pass.

We arrived at Rotterdam abt 8 oclock. After being detained some time at the custom house we took up our quarters at the groote Schiffershuis, a tolerably good inn. Walked out to see the town, which is well built, the houses high and almost all leaning forward, so that the streets at top are actually narrower than at bottom. All the principal streets have canals running through them and generally trees planted on their banks. The inhabitants seemed to be enjoying themselves, much more, certainly, than the common people appear to do in England. The side pavement in the streets is of small bricks.

Monday June 13.[32]

Set out at 6 oclock in a trekschuit [canal boat] for the Hague. This mode of travelling is extremely convenient; the motion almost imperceptible, the rate about 4 miles an hour, the charge moderate, and the variety of scenery as the boat glides along amusing and often interesting. The villages on the banks are the picture of order and cleanliness. Every thing in Holland bears the stamp of the most assiduous industry. The boats, the houses, the roads, the fences, the lands, — everything in short that meets the travellers eye. The boats are all brightly varnished, and appear to be washed daily, almost hourly; the houses a good deal resemble neat English cottages, but the stones of which they are built, are smaller. The roads are paved with these small bricks, with a layer of sand over them; and are nearly as good as our best roads — the lands are every where intersected with small canals, and are d[r]ained after rain by means of windmills which raise the water into the canals; for these are very generally on a higher level than the adjoining fields. From what I have seen of the Dutch in these two days, I shd say that they are a most friendly, good tempered, chearful people; and that they present in their general intercourse with strangers a striking contrast to England. Almost every peasant who meets you, doffs his bonnet and greets you. The proportion of substantial farmers, who live on their own property is very large. Their habitations present the appearance of the greatest plenty, without luxury; and their general character, as Higgins tells me, is that of the greatest independance without pride. Of large landed proprietors there are few; but there are likewise scarcely any beggars: I have not yet seen one. The road passes through Delft to the Hague. There we breakfasted and I then pro-

TO HOLLAND AND TO NEW HARMONY

ceeded in a large gig drawn by two horses, with Higgins to Bennebroek, a village near the Haarlemer Meer, where his sister lives. The road leads through the most beautiful woods and alleys almost the whole way. On the road I was amused by observing the care with which the hay stacks are built. Each stack is covered by a thatched roof, peaked at top, and hung between four poles, which are perforated with holes at regular distances. The roof is connected with these by strong pins, so that it can be moved up and down at pleasure. Many of them are built hollow with an entrance large enough to admit a cart, so as to serve the purpose of a shed: a perfect specimen of the economy of the Dutch.

Higgins' sister[33] appears a most sensible and superior woman. I was particularly pleased with her manner of managing her children and a little nephew of whom she had lately taken charge. I find that I understand the greater part of a conversation carried on in Dutch, particularly when Higgins speaks, to whose voice I am accustomed. I am persuaded that in a month I should understand every word. Slept at Bennebroek.

Tuesday June 14.

Set off about 11 oclock for Haarlem, and arrived just in time to hear the celebrated organ there, the largest and most powerful in the world. We did not hear it played by a great deal so loud as it may be played, yet the sound shook the ground on which we stood though at the distance of more than half the immense Haarlem cathedral. The stop which imitates the human voice is so beautiful that, but for its immense power, it is hardly possible to distinguish it from one. Indeed, when it was first played in a piano passage, I, not knowing that there was such a stop, supposed it was some beautiful female voice accompanying the organ.[34] The cathedral itself is so high that the roof is seen as the first object in approaching the coast over the top of the dühnen [dune] (or natural barrier on the coast).

At Haarlem we visited Madame Bosset [?], a friend of Higgins, and then proceeded in the trekschuit to Amsterdam, where we arrived about 5 o'clock. Amsterdam is a fine airy town, intersected, like all the principal Dutch towns with large canals, with a row of trees on each side. These canals are most useful in transporting merchandise to the very doors of the houses; and give the town in summer a pleasant cool appearance. The houses are beautifully clean, as indeed every where in Holland, and the front doors generally highly varnished and ornamented.

On the road from Haarlem to Amsterdam, we passed a stop where the Haarlemer Meer and the Zuider Zee are not 30 yards apart, separated by two immense sluices, which I believe can be opened at pleasure. From this spot, one sees across part of the Zuider Zee to Zaardam where a complete *forest* of windmills (consisting of many hundreds) is visible. Near to this spot, too is a small bay of the Haarlemer Meer, covering probably 3 or 4 acres of ground, the right of fishing in which is let yearly for 6000 florins (£500).

After dining (at Amsterdam) we went to the French theatre, where I was much pleased with the acting, particularly of a small piece which was played the first, called frère et soeur. The wonderful self command of even the most inferior french actors I admired extremely. Afterwards we supped at Madame Fislers, a particular friend of Higgins.—The manners of the Dutch please me much as far as I have seen them: they appear kind without ceremony, so that one is quite at one's ease immediately. Slept at Fraser's, Higgins' brother-in-law.

Wednesday, June 15.

Went with Higgins, Skene and Madame Fisler to see the blind asylum of Amsterdam. An excellent institution, where blind children are received and taught reading, writing, geo-

To HOLLAND AND To NEW HARMONY

graphy and music, besides various sorts of work. Some of them show a very great taste for music and one of the blind children educated here is now organist in one of the principal churches in Amsterdam. They are taught reading at first by large letters cut in wood, then with smaller types; and at last by a book so strongly stamped with types as to raise the letters on the opposite side: of course a sheet can only be printed on one side. Georgraphy is taught by means of raised maps.

I bought several little things: among others a gamebag and a piece of music composed by one of the pupils. In the music room there are some figures of boys painted over the door so admirably that one has the greatest difficulty in convincing oneself that they do not project.

The passage floors of almost all the houses in Amsterdam are floored with white* marble and the walls a certain way up, the same. Even this blind asylum was floored in this way. It gives the passages a handsome and very tidy appearance.

We then went to the "Felix meritis." A large building belonging to a literary society in Amsterdam, consisting of several hundred amateurs, who meet in winter statedly, sometimes to inspect paintings or copy statutes or living models who place themselves in various positions, naked, for that purpose; sometimes to hear lectures or orations delivered by members of the society on various literary subjects; sometimes to hear a concert, got up in the most superior stile. The society meets for one or other of these purposes every evening throughout the whole winter: and a more excellent institution or one more worthy of being imitated every-where, I do not know. The lecture-room, concert room etc are spacious and well arranged. There is besides a collection of casts from the most superior busts and statues, a collection of various chemical, mechanical and other apparatus and some excellent paintings.

---

* with streaks of grey through it

From thence we proceeded to see a very fine collection of paintings by Dutch and other celebrated masters in the Trekkenhuis.[35] Some of them were most beautiful, far superior to any thing we have in England that I have seen; particularly one of Gerard Dou's[36] (a village school by candlelight) and one by Paul Potter[37] (a landscape with figures of cattle); and some fruit pieces, figures of animals and sea pieces. In one of the fruit pieces was a glass with water, so admirably drawn that the light on it appeared to be reflected from the adjacent window. A large figure of a swan defending its young from a dog, is likewise admirably executed.

Generally speaking, however, the subjects appeared to me to be ill chosen; (sometimes most horrible, for instance the murder of the innocents) : so that the more perfect the execution, the more revolting does the picture become. Most of the other subjects were either unnatural or uninteresting, a circumstance which detracted greatly from the pleasure which paintings so admirably executed were calculated to give.

Dined with Madame Fisler, whose family is most friendly and who appear excellent people.

Went to the German theatre, where I saw Herr Schütz act the part of a father who had become mad in consequence of his harshness having forced his only daughter to elope from him. His acting was, like some of the pictures we had seen, *inimitable*. Every movement, every word and action was perfect and represented in the most faithful manner those of a maniac, who has still some gleams of remembrance and of reason, and the excess of whose paternal feelings had driven him to madness: But still the picture was horrible; so that many females could never, I am told, bear to witness it. The other actors were inferior.

Thursday June 16.

Left Amsterdam in the trekschuit for Muyden. In passing through the streets to the boat, I saw several small carriages

To Holland and To New Harmony

like noddies, but hung very low upon sledges, which I am told are to be seen by hundreds in Amsterdam in wet weather, when the streets become slippery.

On our way to Muyden, we passed several floats of wood drawn along the canal by horses: one of these was full 300 feet long by abt 10 broad, and drawn by one horse only. These are the large floats which come down the Rhine and are thus transported to Amsterdam.

They have a singular method of training their trees before some of the houses here. The lower branches are trained horizontally over a frame work of wood, so as to form a most agreeable shade where the tops project above.

From Muyden we proceeded through Naarden a very strongly fortified town to Baarn, H's native village.

Naarden was fortified by Coehorn,[38] the famous Dutch engineer and is considered nearly impregnable. It is surrounded by a very broad and deep moat which is passed by several wooden bridges, one of which is of rather a peculiar construction. It was found, namely that the stakes which supported the bridge did not decay when entirely under the water, nor rapidly when entirely above: but very rapidly between wind and water (that is just where they met the water, being sometimes wet and sometimes dry). When they decayed there, it became extremely tedious to take out the lower part of the stakes, they being still quite fresh, and to replace them. To remedy this inconvenience, the stakes were all cut off below the water, planks placed over them so as to form a floor, and on this floor the stakes to support the bridge were placed. These being short, were easily replaced when they decayed.

Baarn is most picturesque Dutch village, the cottages, (many of which are large and extremely comfortably, even elegantly filled up inside) appearing through the trees, surrounded by gardens. We lodged at Mr. Fraser's a relation of Higgins', where we were most kindly received; indeed they wd scarcely allow us to depart. I visited with Higgins the cottage in which Penn, the mayor of the village and a particular friend of H's, lives. I should [blank] a most favorable specimen of a class of persons which is in Holland very numerous. That of small landed proprietors[39] farming their own property and living in perfect comfort and plenty, though not in luxury, cultivated, though perhaps not refined, and completely independent, though not in the possession of great riches. I know no class of persons, who appear to me more favorably situated for happiness than this class; almost the only circumstance which appears to me likely materially to detract from their enjoyment, is the continual necessity of driving bargains, in the way of business, with their neighbours. As it is they appear to me an excellent class of people. Penn is a good tempered, open hearted, chearful fellow with a very fine family, shrewd in his conversation, and easy, if not polished in his manners.

At Mr. Fraser's, who is a very sensible and liberal man we met in the evening a very pleasant party, among whom was a lady of the name of Glimmer, from the West Indies. Madame Glimmer speaks English perfectly and seemed quite pleased to find some one who wd speak English to her: some of the young ladies, too, occasionally joined in the conversation in English, which is becoming more common amongst them than it used to be: and with one young lady I conversed for some time in German, which language, to my surprise, she spoke extremely well.

On the whole I was exceedingly pleased with Baarn and its inhabitants. Every where a hearty welcome without any fuss, and real kindness without any ceremony. I scarcely know any place that seemed to me on so short an acquaintance, so desirable a place of residence. I was quite at home; and shall always have the most pleasant associations in connexion with this spot. I wish I could have spent some time here; and then I am convinced these feelings wd have been strengthened daily. Schade dass der arme H. nicht dieselben haben kann. Ihm

TO HOLLAND AND TO NEW HARMONY

sind sie auf immer fuerchte ich, zerstoehrt ud auf welche unglueckliche Weise. [Pity that the poor H. cannot have the same. I fear they are for him forever destroyed, and in what unhappy manner.]

We went, in the course of the afternoon, to Zusdyk, [?] where we saw the princes* Lusthuis, which is neatly, but not expensively furnished, and in which the most interesting object is a painting of the battle of Waterloo, where the prince is represented leading on his troops. This painting is beautifully executed particularly the figure of a wounded man, of a fallen curassier and of the prince and his horse.

After seeing the palace we were proceeding through the gardens, but I found the stomach complaint which I had had a few weeks since about to return and I was obliged to come back to the nearest inn and take a chaise from thence. There I saw the young woman[40] whom Higgins had saved from drowning two years ago.

Friday June 17.

Set off in the Diligence which we met at Zusdyk [?] and after passing through Amersfoort arrived at Appeldoorn, in Gelderen, where we slept. The country through which we passed today a good deal resembles the flat parts of Scotland. There [are] a few inequalities scarcely to be called eminences but which some of our fellow passengers from Amsterdam admired as *large hills*. There is a good deal of wood and some heath and moorland. The horses in Holland are I think on the whole superior in appearance to our English horses. The draught horses are almost all perfectly black, are well-bred, have long manes and tails, (the latter after [often?] tied with bows), and a great deal of spirit. They appear as if they were well kept and not overworked. The diligence at the rate of about 6 miles an hour.

---

* the hereditary prince of the Netherlands

Saturday June 18.[41]

Set out at 2 oclock in the morning for Zwoll and arrived there through rather an uninteresting country and through deep, sandy roads to Zwoll, 26 miles, which we reached about 9 o'clock to breakfast. From thence we proceeded immediately through Meppel to Frederiksoord.[42] The whole of the country through which we passed today is more open and less sedulously cultivated than any we have yet seen in Holland. The soil every where a light sand rendering the cross roads so deep that we required 15 hours, from Appeldoorn to Frederiksoord, a distance of something less than 60 miles, although the vehicle we travelled in was light and the horses strong and spirited.

After dining at the Frederiksoord inn, we walked out to look at the Colony which appears of very considerable extent; the cottages neat, but certainly not elegant, the fields in good order but not bearing very heavy crops. We spoke to one peasant, who asked us to go into his hut with the greatest civility. It was comfortable enough, though small. He informed that there were 81 cottages and abt 900 persons in this colony: and that 4 years ago the spot on which his cottage stood was entirely unreclaimed moorland as the lands beyond it are still; forming the most striking contrast to the fertile fields and neat cottages of the colony.

In passing through I was surprised to find no apparent signs of sociability among the inhabitants. Not a single group, even of children was to be seen. Every thing was perfectly quiet; almost lifelessly so. No sounds either of riot or merriment; no appearance either of disorder or chearfulness was there. Whether the inhabitants might be all assembled, each in his own house, I cannot say. It might be in consequence of its being Saturday evening.

Today we passed through a large district of country which last February was completely under water, as the road

View of a Part of the Colony of Fredericks-Oord

testified by its rough state. In one village through which we passed 17 persons had been drowned and in another 21. Many other villages had lost in much greater numbers.

The inn at Frederiksoord is large and appears to be pretty good.

Frederiksoord

Sunday June 19.

After breakfast we went to the church at Fleddern, a village at about 4 miles distance from Fredericksoord, in order to meet Mülder, a young man whom we had known at Hofwyl as one of Vehrli's[43] pupils, and who is now superintendent of a school at Wateren, (abt 6 miles from here) where some of the most superior children of the colonists are educated as future superintendants, nearly on the same plan as the Vehrliknaben [pupils of Vehrli] in Hofwyl were educated: reading, writing, accounts, botany, singing, gymnastik and the outline of chemistry and mathematics being taught; besides agriculture in theory and practice: the children are 4 hours per

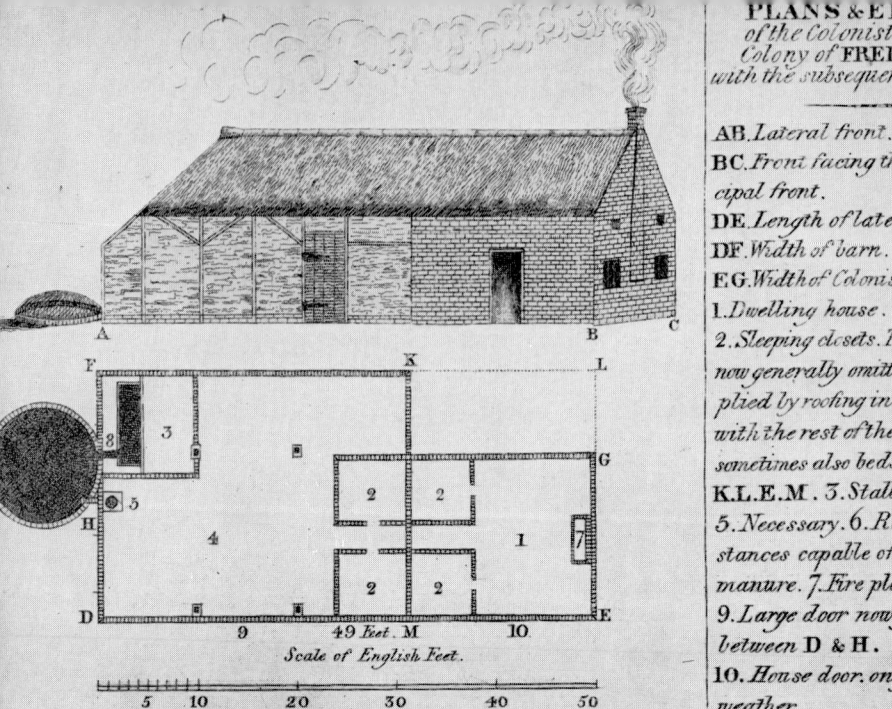

PLANS & ELEVATIO
of the Colonists Houses in
Colony of FREDERICKS-O
with the subsequent improvem

AB. *Lateral front.*
BC. *Front facing the high road*
cipal front.
DE. *Length of lateral front.*
DF. *Width of barn.*
EG. *Width of Colonists dwelling h*
1. *Dwelling house.*
2. *Sleeping closets. Those neares*
now generally omitted, & their pl
plied by roofing in the Portion
with the rest of the house. The
sometimes also beds in the garre
K.L.E.M. 3. *Stalls.* 4. *Barn.*
5. *Necessary.* 6. *Receptacle for*
stances capable of being conve
manure. 7. *Fire place.* 8. *Drai*
9. *Large door now generally p*
between D & H.
10. *House door. only open in*
weather.

day in school and 8 hours in the fields: there are at present 30 or 40, but the number is to be increased to 100.

We found Mülder in coming out of the church, (where we had seen a large congregation of the lower order of peasantry, some from Frederiksoord, others from the neighbourhood). He went with us back to Frederiksoord and gave us a good deal of information regarding the colony, of which the following is the substance:

The "society of benevolence" consisting of members and established about 7 years ago determined to endeavour to suppress pauperism by colonising paupers and orphans; (Each member of the society paying $4\frac{1}{2}$[44] florins, i.e. 4/2d a year, which goes to defray the expenses of the society). In pursuance of their object, the society negociates loans at [blank] p. ct to a considerable amount;[45] and expends these in purchasing bruyères, (i.e. districts of moorland) in bringing the same under cultivation; in building cottages for colonists; in purchasing clothes, implements, seeds, cattle and other necessaries with which they furnish the colonists on their arrival. There are 3 individuals, General van den Bosch,[46]

To Holland and To New Harmony

and 2 others who act as general committee, (or as trustees, I suppose) for the Society; and there is for each establishment a sub-committee of management which superintends the affairs of the colony under their care. This sub-committee builds for each 3½ acres of land, a cottage consisting of one principal room, two or three small closets and a barn and cowhouse: further it prepares the land around this cottage, before the arrival of the colonist; it furnishes him and his family on his arrival with 2 suits of clothes, domestic implements, a cow, one or two pigs, a spade and hoe and some provisions; and with [blank] acre of gardenground, which he is left to cultivate as he likes. It employs the colonists besides at a certain rate of daily wages in cultivating all the land, supplying horses, ploughs, carts and other implements, seeds, manure etc. etc.; thus in fact cultivating each colonists ground for him; and receives from each family for this 50 florins, i.e. £ 4" 3" 4 per year. It leaves to the peasant the produce of his 3½ acres and purchases that part of it from him which he chooses to dispose of at a fixed rate considerably above the market price. This produce is principally rye and potatoes; and from a mixture of these, bread (roggenbrod) is made and retailed to the colonists at a rate to indemnify the committee for the expense of purchase. But for two months in the winter when their wages are insufficient for that purpose they are furnished with bread on paying only the expense of baking, they having previously furnished the committee with an equivalent quantity of rye and potatoes.

Their wages are paid in *tokens* coined by the society, not in money. These tokens enable them to purchase at the society's store, which is established and conducted by the committee; but where they can purchase no spirits. It was found that they exceeded in this respect and *therefore,* as I understand, were these tokens given instead of money.

But when a colonist has shown himself capable of cultivating his own property on his own account he is allowed to do so, and does not then pay the 50 florins yearly. It is found that he is soon able to do so; and to spare time besides to labor for the society, from whom for that labor he, of course, receives wages, as the others do. Before this period, however he must have repaid the sum advanced to him in the first instance by yearly payments. Many colonists have already done so; and are now out of debt.

The society offers to receive into one of the colonies a family not exceeding 6 in number, sent by overseers of parishes or by any public society, or by any private individual, on the payment of *1600 florins* (£ 133" 6" 8) or of *100 florins* (£ 8" 6" 8) a year for 16 years; at the end of which period of 16 years the ground, house etc. shall belong to the overseers or individuals so advancing: and in the meantime the society takes the complete charge of the poor family.

Thus the colonists themselves always remain tenants and can never become proprietors.

The education of the children of the colonists in general is of the ordinary description. They are taught reading writing and something of accounts and singing.

We[47] dined at the inn and proceeded after dinner to take a walk through the colony. We went up to a man who was standing at his door and he very courteously invited us to come in. We did so, and entered into a long conversation with him of which the following was the substance:

He said he was an overseer; and as such earned 10d @ 15d per day, which was paid to him entirely in colonial copper money and paper tokens, which is the only species of money any laborer ever receives from the society and which is current *only* in the society's store: so that every laborer must purchase what he wants there. The natural question was if the articles in that shop were good; to which he replied that many of them were very bad; that he could scarcely drink the tea; that the bread was bad (and he gave us some to taste which in truth fully justified his assertion) that the tobacco was bad; but

To Holland and To New Harmony

that the other articles, such as sugar, salt etc. were very good. No meat was sold in the store at all; nor do the colonists with a very few exceptions ever eat any: their whole food being this wretched roggenbrod and potatoes with tea in the morning; and vegetables from their garden in their season.

He said that not one of the colonists had ever paid the originally contracted debt; nor did he believe that they ever would; that his was originally 229 florins, of which in 4 years being an overseer he had been able to pay 38 florins; which he believed was the most any one colonist had ever paid, most of them getting much deeper into debt, year by year. He said that he paid 50 florins a year for house and land and 100 florins for the working of his land (but I think this was some mistake) and that he paid statedly (I think) 2/6 a week for clothing, which he considered too much. He said he thought all the colonists wd gladly go away if they could; but that they had no money. The plan of his house is here annexed,[48] containing 1 sitting room with one bed, a large light closet with one bed, a small closet and an outhouse where the cows were kept, of which each colonist receives 2 and the produce of which he may sell as milk or butter. He said further that the committee paid 28 stübers i.e. 28d per bushel of rye, the market price being only 18d. And 8d per bushel for potatoes, which is likewise more than the market price; but that the great disadvantage was that this was paid to them only in tokens. On the fields they cultivate only rye, potatoes and flax; oats nor wheat not succeeding. He seemed a decent man, and his house was in appearance above the average.

We afterwards went into house of an inferior description, the occupier of which confirmed what the other had said regarding the articles bought at the store; he said he earned 8d a day; and that he paid 50 florins a year for house and land and 50 florins for cultivation. He *never* on any occasion was able to purchase meat. He considered it out of the question that any colonist shd ever be able to pay his debt. His own debt was originally 207 florins; and this had been increasing year by year since he came (6 years ago) and was now in all 779 florins. He had 3 morgens land one half rye and the other equally divided between potatoes and pasture. His hut was very poor looking and exhibited little apparent comfort. He showed us all his books of reckoning; and allowed us to take an old one with us. He said that he considered the land of so bad quality that *if he were to receive a present* of it, the house and all that was in it and to be freed from debt entirely, *it wd be quite impossible for him, even then, to maintain himself without assistance.* He was very civil, but seemed afraid to say any thing about the management of the committee. We tasted his bread, of which however he did not complain and found it just as bad as the other's. We tasted the water from his well wch was close to the house. Spirits are totally prohibited.

Monday June 20.

Set[49] out at 6 o'clock for Vennhuisen, one of the largest colonies as we heard when [which] is about 18 miles from hence. Passed through Wateren on our way and look[ed] up Mülder who had promised to accompany us. There being 4 in the carriage, I rode.

The country is bleak and in general rather uninteresting and towards the colony it becomes an extended heath, which however I am told is much more productive and consequently more valuable than that at Fredericksoord.

At Vennhuisen we found three large squares of 500 feet each side, one story high, built of [?].[50] The first we came to designated as N 3 is now building. The rooms inside, (consisting of 12 large dormitories, 95 feet by 15, and a few small rooms for superintendants) are preparing for the reception of 960 orphans, 80 in each dormitory. Outside all round the square and separated by a partition wall from these, are small rooms, with 4 beds in each, in the wall, for free colonists, who are to possess no land, but are simply to be employed as

The Agricultural Workhouse at Veenhuisen

laborers: there are abt 30 of these on each side, besides superintendants chambers.

We then proceeded to N 2, at about ¾ mile distant. On the way we passed through a quantity of heath or moorland just preparing for cultivation. The manner of effecting this pursued by the society is as follows: The ground is first plowed; that [then] the turf thus turned up is heaped in very large stacks; and, after standing a few summer months it is burned, and the ashes scattered over the land: then ditches are dug at 72 feet apart, all through land is [in] parallel lines; these ditches are 6 feet broad at top and narrow towards the bottom where they are only 3 feet broad, and they are 4 feet deep. This is found sufficient to furnish sand enough to cover all the land with sand 3 inches deep: the land is then dunged and ploughed and the seed immediately sow[n]; either rye or buckwheat will succeed. The ditches are left as drains. The excavation of these ditches is paid for at the rate of 2d for 100 cubick feet. There are now *6000 acres* of heath in various stages of progression around Vennhuisen. The whole operation till the seed for the first year is sown costs 150 fl per morgen or about 6 guineas an acre. The cakes which remain from rape

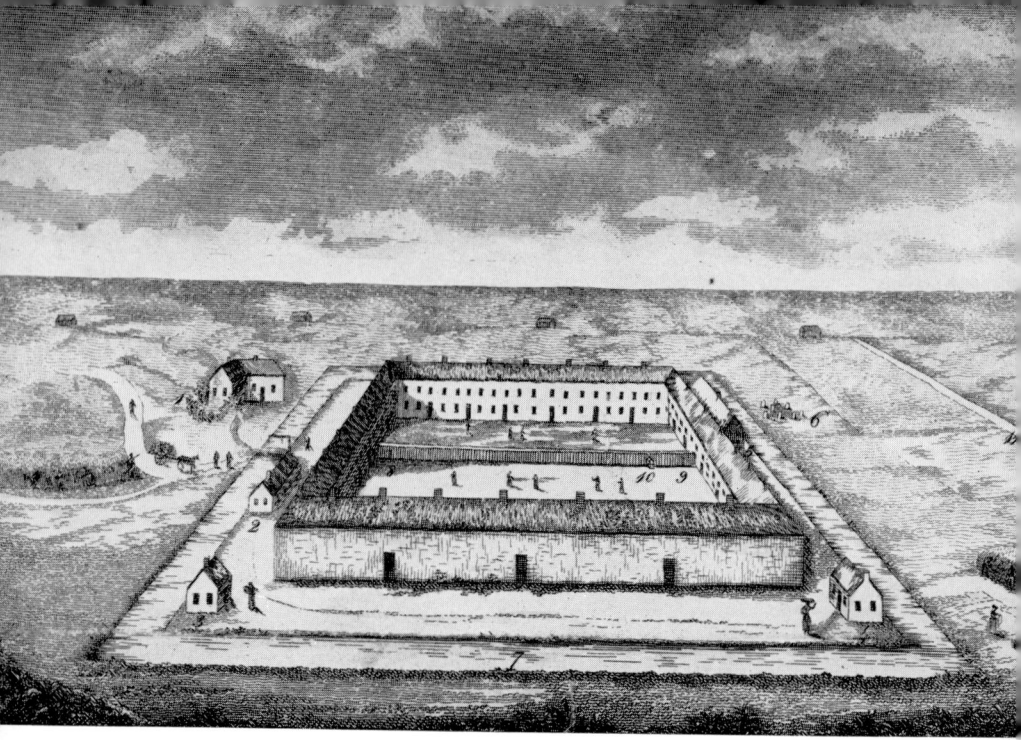

The Agricultural Workhouse at Veenhuisen

1. Subdirector's house 2. Guard house 3. Bake house 4. Washing house 5. Hospital
6. Burial ground 7. Canal 8 and 9. Wall of division between men and women 10. Smithy
11. Farm houses

seed when the oil is expressed, ground to a powder form excellent manure.

The land here, I am told, when cultivated for 3 or 4 years will let for about 5/ an acre.[51] The second square N 2 is filled with beggars and with those who are removed to it in consequence of misconduct in the other colonies and who are here treated in the strictest manner. The square is of the same dimensions and similarly arranged to N 3.

Throughout the whole of the 6000 acres before mentioned, there are large farm houses, occupied by those colonists who in other situations, at Frederiksoord etc, have conducted themselves with the greatest propriety. Each of these farmers has 20 cows and 2 horses. The houses contain a pretty large sitting room, a small milk house, and a large cowhouse. They must furnish the society with 1½ lb butter weekly per cow. The rest is at their own disposal. These peasants are employed as superintendants over the orphans and others; and receive for that 5 guldens or 8/4 per week. With this and the profit of the milk they may be very comfortable. We went into one house and found the family at dinner. This very family, however, had still 300 fl. of the originally contracted debt and which they were still paying up.

In N 2 as at Omerschanz where we go tomorrow, punishments are inflicted on refractory members. Only one instance is known when the individual cd not be brought to work: this was in the case of a woman, who was first confined, then whipt! then put in heavy irons! and finally threatened with death! if she did not work; but she persisted in her refusal and they were obliged to dismiss her. The General seems to have very unlimited power.

The beggars who are apprehended and brought hither are allowed to go free, as soon as they have saved 30 fl. which many of them do very soon; but after doing so, several have applied to remain still. Persons, it is said, who were not beggars and had therefore been refused admittance into this colony, have gone to the nearest village and immediately qualified themselves by begging there.

We then proceeded to N 1, an immense orphan school. It is a square of the same dimensions as the others where 1300 orphans and foundlings are lodged, fed and clothed. They are from 6 up to 18 years of age; at 18 they may choose their own mode of life.

These orphans work in the fields, or in some simple, old fashioned manufacture during 9 hours per day and are besides 2 hours in school. They have 3 meals a day; for breakfast and for supper, butter and bread, and bread and milk; and for dinner some kind of vegetable mess. They sleep in small cots, which during the day are drawn up to the roof, so that the dormitory becomes an excellent dining room. NB. *This plan appears to me to be an excellent one.*

The children though sadly inferior in appearance, are still I think superior to those in the usual orphan schools. The school is most simple, but I think, conducted on excellent principles; something of Pestalozzi in it. The bake house is very large. The bread is 1/3d rye and 2/3ds potatoes. The total expense for each orphan for food is scarcely 1d per day. Their clothes are strong and coarse and all of their own manufacture. This establishment at present *does more than clear its own expenses*.

Before leaving this we met General van den Bosch himself and Mr. Visser the other superintendant to whom we had a letter of introduction. The General with whom Skene spoke, he thought a most intelligent and superior man. Mr. Visser is, I think, a shrewd sensible person, most willing to give every information. He informed that of this immense establishment of Vennhuisen nothing was there *two* years ago. The land was purchased at the rate of from 10 florins to 30 florins per morgen; i.e. for nearly 2 acres; for a morgen contains 600 Rhinish roods of 144 square feet each; i.e. 86,400 square feet or 9600 square yards; an English acre being 4840 square yards. He said that there were now no beggars in Holland, except perhaps a straggler here and there and that was entirely the fault of the magistrate; for as soon as a beggar is found, he is sent to one of the colonies which immediately admit him. Several individuals as before mentioned qualified themselves to enter, when refused. The General explained to us that the occasion of the bad bread which we had tasted the day before was that the water had become bad, which it is liable to do at particular seasons; but that it was already remidied. He said the colonists could not be expected to repay their debt at the present low price of provisions, although if the prices had remained as high as they were, when the thing was first set agoing, they could easily have done so. Most of the public charities of Holland are, probably from interested motives, so averse to send the poor hither, that there are actually 1500 *paid for* who have not been sent. The General says he could receive 10,000 colonists yearly now. Mr. Visser explained to

To Holland and To New Harmony

me that the farmers on the 6000 acres were to be allowed, as soon as the matter was properly arranged to contract for their farms, and then to employ the colonists on them, paying them wages. The general very justly observed that we must not look upon these colonies as anything else but a beginning and a very imperfect one, upon which, however, it was easy to improve, when it was once fairly en train. He seems to be quite alive to the necessity of beginning to improve the wretched condition of the lower classes and of their children *physically* before any moral or mental improvement can be effected. He is going to introduce gymnastics. The cost of food for each child is 1d per day or about 30/ per year; and for clothes and every other necessary 30 florins or 50/; making the total expenses per year for each orphan £4. It is found that this establishment can support itself.

On our way to Vennhuisen, we passed through another colony of very neat and apparently comfortable tiled cottages.

The total expense of erecting such cottages is 500 florins; and the expenses for each family of colonists will be nearly as follows. (6 members)[52]

Purchase of land 6 acres of bruyere	50 fl.
Building house	500
Preparing land for the colonists @ 150 fl per morgen	450
Stock of clothes furniture etc. abt	200
Total	1200 florins.
or £ 100 Sterling	

And the expenses per week of each colonist is about as under: (man and wife and 3 or 4 children)

42 lbs of rye bread @ 1/2 per lb.	–"1"9
3 sheffels (of [blank] lb each) of potatoes @ 6d a sheffel	"1"6
2 lbs of butter @ 5½ per lb	""11
and 2½ florins in money; expended for clothes (say about 1 florin); for tea, buckwheat, salt, etc. etc.	–"4"2
Total per week £	–"8"4

Tuesday, June 21.[53]

Set out at 7 o'clock and proceeded through cross roads leading through pretty rural scenery, to Omerschanz, where there is an establishment to receive beggars and those who have conducted themselves ill in the other colonies. These are lodged in a square of buildings containing one morgen inside. We had a letter of introduction to Mr. Harloff, the director, whom we found to be one of the most intelligent superior characters I have ever met with. Indeed I scarcely remember to have been ever so much pleased with any one on so short an acquaintance. He was 16 years in the army, serving in Spain, Russia etc., until, as he said, he had got enough of it. And now he is settled here; and every thing wears an aspect of chearfulness and order and plenty under his management. He took us over a part of the farm, which had been reclaimed only two years. The crops of rye and of potatoes were some of the finest I ever saw, *in any soil*; and Harloff seemed to take a goodnatured pride in showing it to us. He took us into a couple of cottages, which were the picture of cleanliness and order and comfort. In one of these we found a number of rosy little children sitting round the fire eating a sort of pancake made of buckwheat. I tasted; and I never ate a better pancake in my life. In each of these cottages which contain a good sized sitting room, a large light closet and 2 small milk-stores, besides a large barn and cowhouse, one family lives chosen from among the colonists at Frederiksoord who had conducted themselves the best. Each has 2 horses, 16 cows and 100 sheep; and these produce sufficient manure for 40 morgens (80 acres) of land, which is the quantity attached to each farm. There are at present 18 such farms and the number is to be increased to 24. They have each 5 florins a week, like those at Vennhuisen, and ¾ths of the produce of their cows. This enables [them] apparently to live very comfortably. The cows are always kept in the house and their food laid before them. The method in which the dung is prepared is this: under a covered shed where the sheep are penned everynight a layer of cut turf is laid; the next day the dung of the cowhouse is laid upon this in addition to the dung from the 100 sheep during the night; then another layer of cut turf; the next day another layer of dung and so on till it becomes 2 or 3 feet deep; and then it is cleared out and forms excellent prepared manure.[54]

In general the first crop from the land is potatoes, or sometimes buckwheat.

This establishment of Omerschanz clears its own expenses this third year already, and will doubtless in future prove a source of considerable profit.

From the farm we proceeded to the workhouse, built on the site of an old square fort. At some little distance is a small building neatly and comfortably arranged as an Hospital, where we [saw] several invalids. Nearer to the square is the school which is nearly the same as at Vennhuisen. It is used as a chapel on Sundays, by both Protestants and Catholics; when the Catholics hold mass there, small folding doors are opened, disclosing the altar, crucifix etc.; and these are closed during the protestant service: an instance of religious charity and unanimity worthy of being imitated in less tolerant England.[55]

In the workhouse, the men occupy one half and the women the other. We saw a good many at work at manufactures, trades etc.; but the greater part were at work in the fields, where the women are allowed equally with the men, and where they are found to be equally useful and effective, except in a few of the more laborious operations. Unpleasant language, I am told, is scarcely ever heard amongst them; and punishment is very seldom required; although it is occasionally inflicted (whipping) for obstinate laziness, for running away, and for drinking:[56] which last, Harloff says, is the worst and most common vice amongst them, and indeed amongst the lower orders of the Dutch generally. The wages vary from 2 and ½ fl (2/6d) per week, the lowest, to 5 fl. the highest (8/4). For 2/6 they are supplied with breakfast dinner supper, bed, clothing and any other first necessaries; so that those who gain more may easily save the whole surplus if they desire it; and as soon as they have saved 25 fl. (abt 2 guineas) they are free to leave the establishment, which many of them, however, are unwilling to do. The name of Omerschanz, however, is dreaded by vagrants all over Holland, they conceiving it to be a place, where they must either work or starve. The hours of labor are 10 per day. There are lists of various articles hung up in the various rooms, with the prices annexed; and these the work people may purchase with their surplus money.

Mr. Harloff most kindly invited Higgins and me to come and stay a week at his house; when he promised us all the various account-books etc. in detail; which, had time allowed, would have been very interesting for me. He requested that I wd write to him, to inform him how we proceeded in America; and promised in return to inform me regarding all that was doing in these colonies. I promised to do so; and shall perform my promise; for Harloff is too interesting a person to lose sight of. If he were disengaged, I believe he wd emigrate to the new world.

We left Omerschanz abt 5 o'clock and arrived through an immense common at Zwoll, at 10 o'clock at night. Zwoll is a considerable town with 12,000 inhabitants and well built.

Wednesday June 22.

Set off in the passage boat for Amsterdam. The wind going down the Yssel was right ahead of us, so that we made but slow progress, and did not get out of the river till towards the evening. When we did get out the wind fell and we had almost a calm during the greater part of the night which we passed uncomfortably enough on the benches of the small cabin, (about 9 feet by 8; and scarcely 5 feet high) as there were no beds. The next morning

TO HOLLAND AND TO NEW HARMONY

Thursday June 23.

We found ourselves alongside of an island in the middle of the Zuider Zee. This island is lower than the Zee at high water and is defended all round by dykes, which however do not prevent its being frequently overflowed, to the great danger of the inhabitants who frequently lose their lives on such occasions; and whose only safety consists in taking refuge in the upper stories of their houses. The island is I presume inhabited entirely by fishermen. After creeping along all day, we found ourselves at 7 o'clock in the evening still at a considerable distance from Amsterdam and nearly opposite Naardam; we therefore hailed a fishers boat, navigated by two most picturesque figures of Dutch fishermen, landed near Naardam and proceeded to the town on foot. There we took leave of Skene and Ford, who proceeded to Utrecht next morning; and Higgins and I took a carriage to Amsterdam which we reached at ½ past 11 oclock. Slept at Mr. Frasers, where we found Penn and his daughter Betche.

Friday June 24.

Visited Mr. Henri Fraser and Mr. Fisler (whose address is M. W. Fisler, Baangragt, près du Leidscheplein, à Amsterdam) from whom I took leave, and who gave me the kindest invitations to make their houses my home, if I should again visit Holland, and whose unceremoniously and easy hospitality and urbanity I shall long remember with pleasure. Dined at Mr. Fraser's and set out at 7 oclock in the evening for Haarlem in the trekschuit: arrived there about ½ past 9 and took a carriage to Bennebroek, where we passed the night. The route from Haarlem to Bennebroek, which we passed by moonlight was at that hour as picturesque and romantic as can well be conceived. The air was remarkably mild, not a breath of wind was stirring, the sky was clear and the moonbeams penetrated here and there through the heavy dark foliage of the woods which in many places completely overhung the narrow winding road of soft sand, along which our carriage rolled silently and rapidly. The whole formed a scene to which the mixed gloom and brightness of these ancient and magnificent woods and the perfect stillness which reigned around added an almost magical effect.

We arrived at Bennebroek about ½ past 10, where we found Mr. & Mrs. Fraser—Higgins sister and brother in law. I remarked the construction of the lamp which Mrs. F. uses, as being very good and producing a very mild and pleasant light. It is very similar to ours except that the top cover, instead of being of ground glass is of sheet-iron painted white. This prevents the light from ascending or striking on the eyes, and throws it down on the table and on all the objects around.

Saturday June 25.

Set out after breakfast for the Hague. The veneration with which people here regard *storks* is remarkable. We observed a sort of box built on the top of a church on purpose to receive a nest of them, in which one of these large, sedate looking birds was standing perfectly motionless. The peasants, I am told regard it as a most fortunate omen if these birds build on their cottages.

The high road to the Hague is much more picturesque than any of our English highroads. It is well paved, but narrow and winding through high ancient woods which grow thickly up to the very edge of the road.

At the Hague we found Higgins' father, a lively pleasant gentleman; and walked with him through the magnificent woods which render the environs of the Hague a delightful resort in summer. These woods are interspersed here and there with considerable pieces of water, the banks of which are planted as shrubberies. Here you find, too, rural places of refreshment, where the parties are seated under the shade of some of the finest old trees I ever saw.

We went to see the museum at the Hague,[57] which is well worthy the attention of every stranger. It contains several rooms filled with Chinese and other curiosities, a model of a Chinese town on a large scale, the weapons and dresses and utensils of the North American Indians and other savage nations; a satyr's head and a stuffed mermaid; besides a large collection of remarkable objects from different parts of the world, which we had unfortunately no time to examine, for the rooms were shut half an hour after we got there. We obtained permission, however, to go upstairs to see the paintings, some of which are excellent. Amongst others the famous bull of Paul Potter, his masterpiece, and I suppose the finest painting of an animal that ever was produced; some paintings of flowers placed on ornamented stands, by Van Os;[58] these flowers are the most perfect imitation of nature that can be well conceived; and some bas reliefs on the flower stands were executed in such a manner that I could not for some time believe that they were not actually raised. A figure of a Swiss peasant girl, by Cels[59] struck me, as being one of the most interesting paintings I had ever seen; the expression of the face, and of the whole figure is admirable. Two portraits by Rubens[60] were likewise beautiful. And there were a number of historical pieces superior to any we are in the habit of seeing in our English exhibitions.

After dinner we went to the French threatre, where I saw, for the first time a French tragedy. The acting was good and powerful, but, to my taste sadly overstrained; a carricature of the feelings it was meant to express.

Sunday June 26.

Set out in the diligence at 2 o'clock for Rotterdam. Arrived there at 4. Slept till 7, got on board the steamboat

(Queen of the Netherlands) at 8, and took final leave of Holland after passing a fortnight there most agreeably.

The[61] general opinion which this fortnight's residence there induced me to form of the country and of the inhabitants, was favorable. Whatever persevering industry can do for a country, has been done here. Every thing bears the impress of industry & cleanliness and of comfort. The scenery is uniform, but not uninteresting; beautifully ornamented, picturesque country seats (called wyk, i.e. retreat) appear in the midst of luxuriant woods and gardens, where the owners retire from the bustle of the towns to seek that quiet and somewhat inactive state of repose which appears to characterize the hours of enjoyment of the Dutch; from which again they regularly rouse themselves to that assiduous, but not laborious or violent, exertion which shall gradually free them from the necessity of exerting themselves at all. This appears to be the object which they, in common with almost all our nations, pursue: but the Dutch appear to me to pursue it more systematically, and perhaps at less expense of present comfort than most other nations. They wish to gain money; but they are not inclined to work like slaves to obtain it, nor to stake their whole property in the hope of making large profits. Few large fortunes are made, but there are likewise scarcely any bankruptcies. The Dutch, as far as I have seen of them, are friendly and unceremonious, disposed to be kind to their friends without putting themselves out of their way. I should think them not easily roused to any violent feelings; not quickly elated by success, nor quickly depressed by a reverse of fortune. I think they would make excellent colonists; who wd not rest satisfied till their industry has made them comfortable, and who wd hardly quarrel, without considerable provocation with any of their neighbours.

Our voyage was a very tedious and rather a rough one. A head wind all day which continued next day

·To HOLLAND AND TO NEW HARMONY

Monday June 27.

and prevented us from getting in sight of land till about 3 o'clock. Almost all the passengers were sick. I and two or three others stood it out the best on deck, although there was occasional rain which made it somewhat unpleasant.

Tuesday June 28.

Arrived about 8 oclock in the morning at London, after a most tedious passage of 48 hours. Breakfasted at Plough Court. Called on M. Gibbs, on P. Chapeaurouge and then went to clear at the Customhouse. This was most tedious and unpleasant; and the officers seem to take pleasure, as being "clad in a little brief authority", in making it as disagreeable as possible. Dined with Morgan. Called at Wheatley and Adlard,[62] and looked out a few books for our library. Called on Silvester. Took up my quarters at Bedford Sq-

Wednesday June 29.

Went to the City to see Gibbs—found that bills for £6000 in part payment of Harmonie had been presented at Barclays for acceptance—The partners appointed a meeting on the subject for tomorrow. Called on Goldschmidt[63] (not at home) Morrison and Lepard. Went to the Diorama. The two views are a moonlight view of Holyrood Chapel and a view of the Cathedral of Chartres. They are both inimitably well executed: the illusion produced by the combined effect of the most correct perspective and of the most skilful management of lights, is perfect. In the first view the moon is seen to rise from behind the building & gradually to highten the lights where its rays fall, the stars twinkle: and the whole is managed in so unobtrusive and so natural a manner, that a minute observation is necessary to remark it. Soft music is heard at a distance; and the room in which the spectators sit being darkened, one might imagine oneself transported at once to the spot, and seated amidst the gray ruins and vaulted arches of this ancient chapel half hidden in darkness, half lighted up by the moonbeams streaking through the broken windows and over the mouldering wall—one might fancy all this almost with the feeling of reality, but for the commonplace and often unmeaning expressions of silly wonder, which, generally delivered in country dialect, betray too palpably the vicinity of the metropolis of the world and drag one back against one's will out of the fairy scene into reality. The illusion produced by perspective in the other painting, is very perfect.

Called on Mrs. Stewart; afterwards dined with John Smith and met Mr. Bowring, Mr. Bentham's principal man of business,[64] and a gentleman who had resided some time in New South Wales. He spoke of the climate as being unequalled for mildness and steadiness. There is, in fact, no winter, yet the summer is not oppressively hot. The natives he considers a very fine race, free and happy, but daily deteriorating as they come into contact with European settlers. They resemble the North American Indians a good deal; but do not, like them, torture their enemies; nor are their wars so sanguine. They are personally finely formed and extremely active. They are but very thinly scattered over the country, a *nation* seldom consisting of more than 50 or 60 individuals. Yet each nation has its own hunting grounds upon which a neighbouring nation may not trespass, without permission, or without giving rise to immediate hostilities.

Thursday June 30.

Breakfasted with Morgan. Attended the meeting of the partners: and found that since yesterday additional bills to the amt of £12,000 had been presented, making in all £18,000. These and one of £2000 which was still to be presented the partners authorized Barclays to accept; acting a friendly and liberal part in this matter. Called on Jones of the India house; not at home. Called on Mr. Slaughter, Leicester Sqr, who received me most kindly. Called on Harding;[65] not at home.

TO HOLLAND AND TO NEW HARMONY

Returned to Bedford Sqr and went with John and Charles Walker[66] to the opera, where we heard Velutti, the soprano singer (ein Verschnittener [a castrate]). The effect of his singing in solos I did not like, as being unnatural and in my opinion quite inferior to a good female voice; but in a duett with a female voice, the effect is very good. The exhibition is doubtless in very bad taste; but it is a phenomenon interesting to see and hear for once. He was received with a mixture of loud applause and hissing.

Friday July 1.

Breakfasted with Mr. Lepard. Saw Völker, who does not appear to be getting on very well. Looked out a few books. Called on Mrs. Wheeler, who was not at home. Called on John Abel Smith[67] who has had the smallpox but is now recovering. Called on Mrs. Kemmis, who particularly requested me to write to her from America and said her brothers address, 16 Upper Grosvenor St., Grosvenor Square would always find her. Dined at Bromley with Jos. Foster, to whom I gave a long Account of Frederiksoord, in which he was much interested.

Saturday July 2.

Rode out to breakfast at Arno's Grove.[68] Called on Mrs. Walker who was at her son Isaac's house about a mile from thence. Bathed in the New River. Returned to town and went to hear the Appollonicon,[69] which is a most powerful and at the same time a most beautiful instrument. The piano passages were executed with the utmost sweetness and precision; and some of the forte passages shook the room, and the window panes with considerable violence. Called on Harding, who is to be in Scotland in three or four weeks; and on Silvester and Hart, neither of whom were at home. Dined at Bedford Sqr drank tea at Plough Court and went off by the Blackwall stages for the City of Edinburgh steamboat, on board which I

215

arrived a little before 11. Fine moonlight evening and very pleasantly mild. Went to bed and slept most comfortably.

Sunday July 3.

Weather beautiful and what little wind there was, fair. Sea calm and continued so all day. Wrote my journal which I had not had time to continue in London, read and walked the deck. Accommodations very good and victuals excellent.

Monday July 4.

Weather fine, but wind, which had freshened in the night contrary. Read. Continued my journal. Played at chess with John Arch Campbell,[70] whom I happened to find a fellow passenger with me.

Tuesday July 5.

Although the wind had continued a head all night, yet at about 8 oclock in the morning we passed the bass rock; and before 11 o'clock, we anchored opposite the Newhaven pier. Got up to Edinburgh. Lodged at Mrs. Moffat's. Called on Dr. Yule, Abram Combe, Mrs. Campbell. Dined with Mr. Small.

Wednesday July 6.

Set out at 6 oclock per Lanark Coach and arrived safely at Braxfield about ½ past 10—Found my mother[71] and sisters[72] well: and all things going on as usual.

* * * * * * * * * *

Sunday July 10.

Received a letter from Skene, dated Brussels, July 2, of which the following is an extract.
"After leaving you, I proceeded next day to Utrecht, "a more lively, busy-looking town than we had yet seen; "staid there half a day and went to visit an establishment of

To Holland and To New Harmony

"Hernhouters[73] at Zeist; was fortunate enough to get hold "of a teacher who spoke German and was communicative. The "establishment consists of two buildings, facing inwards with "a fine avenue between them, thus:

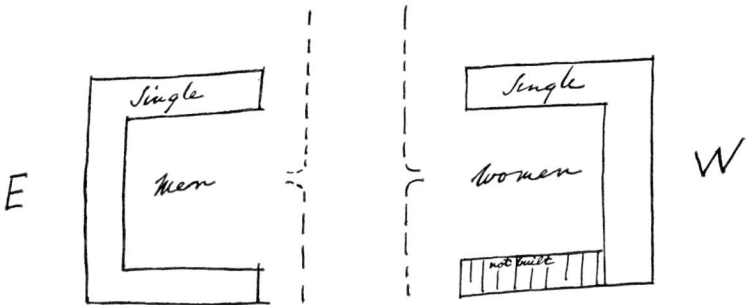

"A little garden ground at the upper end is all the land; a part "of which is laid out as a cemetery. The males are buried on "one side of the garden, the females on the other.

"The number of inmates is at present about 300. 24 "pupils, boarders and 12 pupils from the neighbourhood form "the school. In the south wing of the male building are 60 "single men; and as that wing is 5 stories high there is spare "room for 10 shops on the groundfloor; kitchens, cellars, "baking, brewing etc. below. Above are sitting rooms in which "the brothers pass their leisure hours, 4 & 6 in a room; and in "the attick are the dormitories. The rest of the men's building "is filled with married brothers. There are 100 single women "in their building, and their dining room is on the ground floor "at the west end. Their affairs are managed by a committee "of 12, a vorsteher [superintendent] and a preacher. An "inspector reports to Hernhout in Bohemia. The lodging and "dinners are furnished by the community; and the latter is "paid for by 5 florins (say 8/4) per month, but you may have "choice of wine, en payant. Your dress, bedding, supper etc. "etc. are at your choice, and according to your means. Master "tradesmen receive loans for purchase of materials, journeymen "are paid wages per job; and all articles made are sent to "the shops, and sold at labelled prices. Singing is taught, "marriage is allowed with consent of committee, and by choice "of persons. Manners chearful and lively. Individual wealth "to any amount.—At Antwerp got a note from M van Bree to "the directeur of the colonies at *Voorsel,* and went by the dili- "gence of Turnhout for 4 francs.

"At the colony we visited at least a dozen houses, and "found them arranged like those at Frederiksoord; but better "built and furnished, and the people much cleaner, more "cheerful and better fed. We ate of their good rye bread; and "they told us that they had often butcher's meat. They have "been there from 2 to 3 years only; 70 houses now inhabited "and many more ready. The men were all at work, defrichant "[clearing] the land round a quadrangle for beggars 680 "feet by 466, not yet inhabited. The brother of Genl Van Den "Bosch is a director, and full of good sentiments. He took "much interest in cooperative proceedings and is to hear from "me of our progress. *He regrets that any detached cottages* "*were built,* and has stopped the building of them. Near the "Kasteel, (as they call the quadrangle) are 12 farms, better "than those of Ommerschanz. Paper money, & small current "coin are used.

"The Baron de Keverberg, when in England, committed "to Lord Grenville's charge his book for yr father. He is "here, and told me this morning that the condition of the "colonists at Voersel is so much better than that of common "labourers (who are honnêtes peres de famille [good family "men]) that the committee are going to retrench some of "their small comforts; as 'cela n'est pas juste', says he, 'que "des mendians qui ont été pauvres pour le plupart par leur "propre faute soient mieux etc etc' [it isn't fair that beggars "who have been poor for the most part through their own fault "should be better off etc. etc.] Although their produce is "amply sufficient to cover the annual expenditure and repay

TO HOLLAND AND TO NEW HARMONY

"the interest and capital of the 4800 florins expended in "establishing each house or menage. He says that he has "observed a falling off in his late annual visits to Frederik- "soord, which he attributes to the increased occupations else- "where of Genl. V. d. B. The soil here at Voersel is similar to "that at Vennhuisen."

Monday July 11th.

Heute hatte ich ein langes, sehr interessantes und hoechst befriedigendes Gespraech mit meiner Mutter. [Today I had a long, very interesting and highly satisfying conversation with my mother.]

Tuesday July 12.

Went down to Glasgow, and called on Hamilton[74] on my way down.

Found the booksellers, tailor etc. with their commissions not yet completed, although they, each, promised to have them finished a month ago.

Wednesday July 13.

Staid in Glasgow, looked over books etc.; and found considerable inaccuracy in Wardlaw and Cunninghames accounts. They appear to be very indifferent men of business. Staid at Mr. Wrights.[75]

Thursday July 14.

Returned by Dalzell, where I staid some hours; and went with Mr. Hamilton to Orbiston, part of which is now 3 stories high, part 2 stories, part 1 story, and the foundations of nearly half the building are already laid. It is plainly, but I daresay substantially enough built. One room is to be appropriated to each family. The public buildings to be in the centre thus

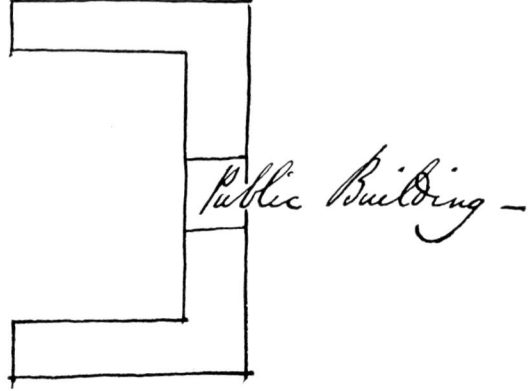

Mr. H. expects to complete one half the masonwork this autumn. And the rest next spring.[76] Settled with Peddie.

Saturday July 16.

In the afternoon had an excellent game at cricket, all the masters of the school attending.

Sunday July 17.

Beautiful day. Took a walk with Barry and Norton to the other side of the river up to Bonnington fall. We descended at Corra Castle, went along the rocks and ascended to the walk nearly opposite Bonnington fall, at the risk of our necks.[77] We were not aware of the danger previously to attempting to ascend, or we shd not have exposed ourselves to it.

Monday July 18.

Had a cricket match with the masters at 5 oclock in the morning: a beautiful morning and a noble game we had. After which I went to the stable for an hour to continue the instruction I am receiving from George in the grooming etc. of Horses; that I may be able to act as my own groom in America when necessary.

To Holland and To New Harmony

Tuesday July 19.

Set out on an excursion to Rosslyn Castle. The party consisted of my mother, Anne, Jane, Mary and Margaret;[78] and Mr. Barry, who has been giving lectures on chemistry to the villagers.

The day was very hot indeed. We proceeded through Biggar and Noblehouse, where we dined to Roslin, where we had previously by letter bespoke beds. But found on our arrival that they had no beds in the inn there at all, so that we [were] forced to [go] on to Lasswade 2 miles further, and being there again disappointed of beds we went on by a hilly dark road to Dalkeith and arrived there about ½ past 11 oclock, having made 40 miles in all, I on horseback, Mr. Barry and one of my sisters in a gig and the rest in our carriage. In approaching Lasswade, the postillion mistook the road and getting into a cross bie road, he brought the carriage down a narrow and very steep part of it, at the risk of the necks of the party.

We found pretty good accommodations at the crosskeys Inn at Dalkeith.

Wednesday July 20.

After breakfast, we proceeded to see Dalkeith House, the seat of the Duke of Buccleugh: a fine plainly built and plainly but elegantly furnished house with some good paintings by Claude Lorraine,[79] Sir Joshua Reinolds[80] etc.: amongst others a set of beautiful views in Venice and Naples by an Italian artist. The museum and billiard room are in one, a very good idea, in my opinion: the museum is small, but the specimens are beautiful preserved, particularly the birds which constituted the greatest part of it. There is close to the house a magnificent amphitheatre of evergreens, surrounding a bowling green and terminated on one side by a neat small bridge over the North Esk.

From Dalkeith, we proceeded again to Rosslin, through Loanhead. There were a great many parties of all descriptions at Roslin, which destroyed the privacy of the place considerably. The castle is certainly a fine old ruin, but two stories of subterraneous vaults are all that are now complete; the rest of the castle having been burnt by Oliver Cromwell; the view down the Esk is very pretty.[81] The chapel[82] which is close to the Inn, is small but richly carved and in good preservation. The carvings, illustrative, principally of Scripture History are in the most grotesque stile; and they were rendered still more ludicrous by the pompous mechanical tone of the set speech in which each of them was explained to us by a complete original, who showed us the chapel; and who exclaimed in the bitterest terms against "that rascal John Knox", who deserved to have been hung up a hundred times for throwing down the twelve beautiful statutes of the apostles from the 12 nitches which still remain, and which he showed us as a monument of this piece of barbarism, as he called it.

We visited the woods of Hawthornden[83] which in my opinion much resemble Cartlane Craigs,[84] though the rocks are not so high; and after dining and eating some Roslin strawberries and cream, we proceeded to Edinburgh and put up at the British Hotel, Queen St, which we [Ms. blank] a most elegant and comfortable hotel, but rather expensive.

Thursday July 21.

After breakfast and after having executed a few commissions, we proceeded towards Lanark on our return; but my mother who had been much indisposed during the morning, found herself so ill, that we were obliged to return and indeed to remain a couple of hours at a small house by the roadside. My mother finding herself rather better, we proceeded to Leith to await Mrs. Stewart's arrival. Bathed. Put up at Mrs. Simpsons, comme ça.

To Holland and To New Harmony

Friday July 22.

After looking out for the steamboat Soho, by which my aunt was expected, all morning, she came in sight about 4 o'clock in the evening. I went on board and brought her and her family on shore. I happened to steer the boat myself, returning, through rather a rough sea, my first essay in that way, in which I succeeded tolerably, —at least brought them all safe to land, after a slight *ducking*.

Saturday July 23.

Returned to Braxfield by Cansycud. The day was pleasant and we arrived in safety about 9 o'clock.

July, August and September were beautiful months in Scotland, the thermometer during nearly a fortnight at one time ranging from 75 to 83, and there was scarcely any rain during the whole time. I employed principally in preparing for our Journey to America, the greater part of it. The teachers Mr. Applegath[85] and I bathed almost daily and improved our swimming much by so doing. In the evening we generally had a game at cricket, which we all enjoyed extremely, and which I consider to have been more efficacious in improving the characters and feelings of our teachers than any other circumstance by which they have been surrounded. It promoted, in a most agreeable and remarkable manner the harmony and liberality which are the foundation of all pleasant social intercourse: and all feelings of a quarrelsome and unaccommodating [Ms. blank] diminished daily under its influence. It has tended more fully to confirm the opinion I previously entertained, that public games have a great and most beneficial influence in forming the character of a community and that on that account they ought to be generally introduced and sup--ported.

We sent our heavy luggage on before, per steam packet to Liverpool (contained in 25 packages) including our library of about 1400 volumes.

Tuesday 27th Sept. 1825.

Left Braxfield at 7 o'clock and proceeded in our carriage accompanied by Mr. Applegath and my sister Anne to Douglas Mill, where we breakfasted. At ten occlock the Herald coach arrived from Glasgow and I proceeded in it along with Mr. Wright through Beattick where we dined, to Carlisle where we arrived at about one half past 6. Here all was bustle and confusion, for it was the race week, and Carlisle was crowded to excess. The day had been beautiful and the scenery, which improves the further one proceeds south, was seen to great advantage. I remarked a beautiful view of Moffat looking back upon it from the road.

At Carlisle we got into the mail and travelled all night towards Lpool. The road is excellent and we proceeded at the rate of about nine miles an hour including stoppages all the way. The night was beautiful, full moon and slightly inclining to frost. I was very unwell during the greater part of the night, but recovered towards morning.

Wednesday 28 Sept. 1825.

Arrived at L'pool about half past 8, and put up at the Talbot Inn. Breakfasted and went to see the New York, where we found a party of Italian singers from the King's opera in London, including Signor Garcia and his wife and daughter,[86] come to engage births: and they seemed anxious to have some which my father had looked at and thought of taking. As no letter had arrived from my father up to the date he promised to write, the Captain was obliged to give these births up to them, and we shall be obliged to take others close to the stern of the vessel where the motion is much greater, and the accommodations are less complete. We then went to the Rathbones counting house where we found Richd Rathbone and afterwards his brother Wm, both of whom were kind and attentive in the extreme in forwarding the various arrange-

To Holland and To New Harmony

ments necessary in shipping our luggage etc. Wm Rathbone went with me to the entrance to the harbour where, as it was just high water, we had a magnificent view of probably upwards of 100 vessels of various sizes going down the Mersey. Nothing could exceed the effect produced. Dined and spent the evening with the Rathbones.

Thursday 29 Sept. 1825.

This day was occupied in passing our goods at the Customhouse, and in procuring the draw back on the books we were exporting, which after considerable difficulty I obtained to the amo[un]t of about £23 nett. Mr. & Mrs. Hunt (Mr. Hunt is, I believe nephew of Leigh Hunt of the Examiner) dined with us. Hunt is a very intelligent and well informed young man, with the most rational and liberal ideas, quite with us, and I think both he and his wife, an interesting young woman, to whom he has just been married, seem much inclined to join us in America, if their family arrangements would permit it. My father arrived at ½ p 9.

Friday 30 Septr.

Continued to pack up and sent the greatest part of our luggage on board.—There was no delay or difficulty in regard to the custom house at all. All that was necessary was to make oath that the articles were for private use and not for sale.

After dinner Mr. & Mrs. Hunt called, and drank tea with us. After tea we went to William Rathbones, where we met Mrs. Walker who is going out with us in the New York. She is a quaker lady who resided for some time amongst the Indians for the purpose of converting them. She seems a very original character, but she did not appear to me a very rational one.

Saturday 1 Octr.

Got the rest of our luggage on board, and got on board ourselves about ½ p 12, when the vessel got out of dock. Beautiful weather and a fine wind which carried us out of the river most rapidly.

Part of our luggage which was to come by a steamboat from Greensch did not arrive in time. We were therefore obliged to let George remain for them, to come out by the William Birnes, which is entered to sail on the 4th Inst. The maidservant we expected did not come, in consequence of suspicious conduct just before she was to have set off.

We lay to off L'pool for a couple of hours to wait for the Captain and some luggage which had not come forward. The wind continued favorable but rather light all day.

At dinner the Captain explained to us the very great use of the barometer at sea. A sudden sinking of the mercury indicates almost to a certainty a sudden gale. In two different instances, he said, he believed his ship to have been saved in that way, in consequence of indicating an appoaching tempest at a time when the wind was perfectly light and the weather remarkably fine.

In the evening our Italian party amused themselves by singing what I supposed to be Italian catches, glees and humorous songs, in the highest spirits, apparently extemporizing with the most perfect ease and harmony. Amongst other amusements they imitated the Scotch bagpipes to perfection. In the next room was Mrs. Walker and her female friends, whose conversation cd be overheard at the moment we were listening to the Italians and formed the most striking contrast that can be supposed.

Sunday 2d Octr.

Wind fair. Got through the North channel which was the road we took, most rapidly. This channel being very narrow, its navigation, except by clear weather and fair wind is dangerous.

At 12 Mrs. Walker held divine service, read a couple of chapters from the Bible, prayed etc. Her manner and intonation are most peculiar and sometimes almost ludicrous; impressive only from her evident sincerity and earnestness in the cause.

From Monday the 3d Octr. till about the 15th we had a succession of gales at first from the SSW and afterwards from NNW. which obliged to lie to during a great part of the time and occasioned many ludicrous scenes during dinner and at other times. One day just in the middle of dinner a sea fell on the cabin skylight, broke two or three panes of glass, flooded the table and in a twinkling dispersed the company, 3 or 4 of them being thoroughly drenched. At another time half a dozen passengers were engaged in a long argument on naval tactics with the captain when a sea fell on their heads and wetted every one of them to the skin to the great amusement of those who were snug below.

After the 15th the weather cleared up, and everything assumed as different an appearance as can be well supposed. The ladies made their appearance, we had music after dinner, and gymnastics and other games during the day. On the 18th a newspaper entitled "The Sextant" was first published, and continued three times a week, which afforded much amusement.[87]

The barometer indicated the various changes with great accuracy.

On the 1st Nov. we were in latitude 41 and longitude 66, having had tolerably fair and generally light winds.

On the voyage we did not speak any vessels, though during the night we passed within a few hundred yards of a vessel which we did [didn't] discover till she was alongside of us.

My father had various arguments in public and private, wodurch er aber nach meiner Meinung nicht viel bewirkte. Es scheint mir dass er sich auf zu heftige ud dogmatische

Weise ausdrueckt ud zu allgemein ist in seinem Tadel der gegenwaertigen Systems. Solch allgemeiner Tadel ist nicht nur ungerecht sondern reizt fast alle diejenigen auch die andere Ideen haben Er neight in den selben Fehler verfallen den er in anderen tadelt. Der groesste Theil unserer Schiffsgefaehrten waren nicht geistreich. Der Sohn des Garcia war wohl der geistreichste von allen ud seine Schwester war auch nicht ohne groesste Faehigkeiten. Der Junge G. scheint hoechst geneigt nach Harmonie zu komen. [whereby however in my opinion he did not accomplish much. It seems to me that he expresses himself in too vehement and dogmatic a manner and is too general in his criticism of the present system. Such general criticism is not only unjust but it also irritates almost all those who have other ideas. He tends to fall into the same fault which he criticizes in others. The majority of our shipmates were not smart. The son of Garcia was about the smartest of all and his sister also was not without great abilities. The young G. seemed most inclined to come to Harmonie.]

 After the 1st Novr we had light gales and on the 4th and 5th a dead calm. However on the night between the 5th and 6th we made land and the next morning found ourselves off Sandy Hook, having had a 36 days passage, which is about the average of the packets of that line — Our passage was on the whole a very pleasant one: our passengers were 41 in number including Messers Barclay and Lynch of New York, Camac of Philadelphia, Hayward of Charleston, and Messers Rodgers, Chartres, Lawrie, Hamilton and daughter, Downing and lady, Prime (of N. York) etc from different parts of the Union: besides Signor Garcia and his party—We had a great deal of amusement of various kinds on board, and everything passed off well. The captain is an intelligent man and I think an excellent seaman. The passengers voted him a gold snuffbox in testimony of their satisfaction.

 The wind being light and contrary on the 6th, we did not approach the narrows till about 6 oclock. In the meantime

To Holland and To New Harmony

the captain had procured us a steamboat, in board which we embarked and arrived at New York about 8 oclock. As it was already quite dark, we did not see anything of the city, which I regretted, as I am told the view on approaching New York is very beautiful.

November 7.

While we were at breakfast this morng Dr. Price[88] to our great surprise came in and gave us the latest news of Harmony. These were, in general, favorable, though the impression here is, that a number of the members are indolent and that this has created very great dissatisfaction among the rest; and that in short the establishment, in a pecuniary point of view, is in a fair way to go to pieces. I dare say there is *some* truth in regard to these complaints, though they are no doubt much exaggerated.[89]

We spent great part of the day in getting our things cleared at the custom-house and in seeing Jeremiah Thompson[90] and some other of my fathers friends. In the evening we went to the Canal Celebration ball, where we found, I suppose, between 2000 and 3000 persons. Saw De Witt Clinton,[91] who has been the principal promoter of this great undertaking.

November 8.

Wrote letters for Europe. My father went to Jericho in Long Island, to visit Elias Hicks,[92] the leader of the unitarian quakers here—we called on Jacob Harvey, on Mr. Thomas and some others. After dinner went to Castle Garden, which is very beautifully situated beyond the battery on the point of land enclosed by the North and East Rivers.

The Castle Garden is apparently a sort of fortification, at present fitted up as a pleasure garden. From it there is a fine view down the east river and of the entrance of the north river, the water immediately in front of the garden being sufficiently deep for the largest vessels. The interior is fitted up like a circus in the interior of which we saw a bear and several eagles. We likewise saw two Indian boys about 12 and 14 years of age, who were shooting with considerable skill at small marks, consisting of knives, gloves etc which they obtained when they shot them down off a small post. Afterwards we went to the theatre with Dr. Price and several of his relations, Mrs. Sisterre, and two daughters[93] Mrs. Fisher[94] and two other ladies. William Tell and the Maid and Magpie. Mr. Hamblin acted in the first and Mrs. H. in the second, both with great effect.

November 9.

After breakfast Mr. Geo Barclay called and gave us a kind invitation to dinner. We then went to make several calls and afterwards escorted Madame and Mademoiselle Garcia to the City Hall a fine building, containing a court of Session and several good but not large rooms. We saw in one of the rooms De Witt Clinton to whom McDonald[95] introduced the Garcias. We afterwards went with them to Mr. Griscom's school in Broad-way,[96] but found the children just being dismissed, so that we agreed to return next day. After dinner we called at Mrs. Sisterre's and on Mr. Hulme.[97]

Went in the evening to drink tea with Mr. Wilkes, Hudson Square, where we met a pleasant party.

Thursday November 10.

Made arrangements to get our large packages landed out of the New York—

After dinner called on the Governor (not at home) and on Mr. Wilkes; and then went to the Luncheon, which is the name given to an evening party of lawyers and literary men who meet for conversation.

To Holland and To New Harmony

Friday November 11.

Set out at 6 oclock per steamboat for Philadelphia and sailed through the Sound, or strait between the mainland (New Jersey) and Statten Island, then up the Raratan a small winding river to New Brunswick. Here we took stages (4 horses each, 9 inside passengers and one beside the driver) 25 miles to Trenton on the Delaware. The country not particularly interesting. The stages coming up with others of the opposition line raced most furiously to the manifest endangering of the passengers necks—The horses are excellent and seemed to enter fully in the spirit of it, and the drivers never used the whip at all. The drivers are very skilful, but this does not prevent accidents: indeed a young man who came into the stage half way, told us that in consequence of two of the stages racing the previous day he was overturned and several passengers were a good deal hurt. Went down the Delaware in the Trenton, an excellent boat which it is said, will go 15 miles an hour with wind and tide in her favor. Arrived at Philadelphia at ¼ before 5 having made the Journey of more that 110 miles in 10 hours and ¾ without any fatigue, for 2 dollars! We certainly have not better travelling anywhere in England. Dr. Price his sister and Mrs. Fisher went with us. Called on S. Spackman.[98]

Saturday November 12.

Made various calls in Philadelphia; saw Mr. Hulme, Dr. Rush,[99] and at the Academy,[100] Maclure,[101] Say,[102] Reuben Haynes[103] and some other members. Philadelphia is regularly and in general handsomely built, of brick with marble steps to all the principal houses. The streets cross at right angles, are wide, and pretty well paved. I have never seen any town in which there appeared to me a larger proportion of a respectable middle class, not extravagant in their expenditure, but living in great comfort in a plain simple stile. The United

States' Bank is a beautiful building, almost a literal model of the Parthenon at Athens. Dined at Mr. Smith's,[104] where my father had a long discussion with several leaders of the Society of Friends, with which they seemed on the whole to be pleased.

Sunday November 13.

Breakfasted with Mr. Hulme, who shewed us and explained to us the excellent and abundant manner in which Philadelphia is supplied with water: nothing can be more complete or convenient. Walked out with Dr. Price to see Madame Fretageot,[105] where we found Leseuer,[106] Maclure, Mr. & Mrs. Lewis and some young ladies, Mrs. F's pupils. M. F. ist eine hoechst sonderbare Frau, scheint ein wahres maennliches Gemueth zu haben, ud ich glaubte sie wird in Harmonie ihren Platz aufs aller beste fuellen; doch davon mehr nachher. [Mme F. is a highly remarkable woman, seems to have a truly mannish disposition and I believe she is going to fill her place in Harmony at her very best. But more of this later.] Dined there and returned in the evening.

Monday November 14.

Wet morning. My father went to Wilmington early, to see those persons there who are desirious of forming themselves into a community. After breakfast went to a public court, and declared my intention of becoming an American citizen. Wrote advertisement for work people, which we then inserted in all the Philadelphia papers. Called on Camac and others. Went in the evening to the Athenaeum,[107] and thence to the museum which is conducted by the Peales[108] and is really very well worth seeing. Amongst other fine specimens, there is a complete skeleton of a mammoth, the only perfect one, I am told, in the world. It is abt 12 feet high. There are a number of little scientific amusements, well arranged, and

TO HOLLAND AND TO NEW HARMONY

which, I daresay, attract many youngsters hither. Some of the stuffed birds are excellent.

Tuesday November 15.

Wrote letters etc. after breakfast. Saw the Pennsylvania bank. Camac went with us to the Philadelphia bank and to see a handsome Episcopalian church. In the evening Maclure and Say called; and we had a long and interesting conversation with them. Went to Dr. Rush's evening party; comme ça: met Miss Roche.[109]

Wednesday November 16.

Set out for New York at 6. A little wet but cleared up. It has only rained twice for a few hours each time since we arrived in this country. Arrived at ½ p 5.

Thursday November 17.

Got our goods out of the Wm Birnes and shipped them on board the Phoenix, Jenkins, for New Orleans.

Friday November 18.

At the Customhouse to get a certificate for our goods, to pass them at New Orleans. This was attended with considerable difficulty, as we unpacked and altered the marks of several of the packages.

At 11 oclock we had a public meeting in the City Hall. Mein Vater tadelte aufs haerteste das bestehende System wie es mir schien auf eine zu heftige und unbedingt aufreizende Weise; doch hat das gesammte Volk Alles sehr gut aufgenommen, und selbst die Stellen applaudiert, die sie am haertesten trafen. Den Eindruck, wuerde nach meiner Ansicht, zehn mal staerker sein, wenn mein Vater verstaend wie er sprechen sollte. [My father criticized hardest the existing system as it seemed to me in a too vehement and absolutely irritating manner. However all the people have accepted it all very well, and have

233

even applauded the parts which hit them hardest. But the impression would in my opinion be ten times stronger if my father understood how he ought to talk.] Very cold today. Dined at Jeremiah Thompson's, where a long discussion ensued between my father and a Mr. Macfarlane.[110] Fouchters und nicht sehr gut geführt. [Fruitless and not very well conducted.] Called on Mr. Post.

Saturday November 19.

At the Customhouse and shipping all day. Dined at Mr. Clibborns.

Sunday November 20.

Visitors all morning. Mr. Hulme and a friend of his, an intelligent woolen-weaver, who thinks of going to Harmony, 3 carpenters who go to Harmony. A very little snow. Went out to walk. Called on Mrs. Sketchley[111] whom my father had seen with her daughter at the meeting on Friday. Drank tea with Captn. Bennett.

Monday November 21.

Effected insurance of goods to New Orleans. Called on Jeremiah Thompson. Several applications to go to Harmony. Dined with Geo. Barclay, where I met amongst others two Mexicans, one of whom was the most complete instance of a regularly educated commercial man I have met with. He rejoiced in the line of life we [he?] had been trained to, as giving, by a regular series of gambling transactions, a pleasant excitement and constant stimulus to the mind; besides when successful, the pleasure felt in outwitting other by superior prudence and ability. A strange instance of the power of education.—Called again on Mrs. Sketchley.

Tuesday November 22.

Off at 6 for Philadelphia. Stopped at Joseph Buonapartes, whither we were conducted by his nephew Charles Buonaparte

To Holland and To New Harmony

(Lucien's son)[112] who seems an excellent, intelligent, and unaffected young man. He has lately published a work on Ornithology, a copy of which he gave my father. The situation of the old house, which was burnt down, is very fine, overlooking the Delaware and all the adjacent country—By the destruction of this house an immense number of valuables, including many beautiful paintings, were destroyed. Found Madame Charles at home, die etwas langweilig scheint [who appears to be somewhat tiresome].

Wednesday November 23.

Charles Buonaparte drove us over the greater part of his uncle's grounds which are very finely situated and tolerably extensive.

Returned to breakfast—Joseph is a fine-looking man, sometimes he appeared strikingly like his brother, dignified in his manners, but quiet, and a little reserved. His house is arranged en palais with antichambers etc; and he is served in considerable stile.

After breakfast he entered into an animated conversation in which he expressed his opinion that his brother's conduct was the result of his peculiar situation, and that Buonaparte was naturally mild and even philosophically disposed.

From Joseph Buonparte's we returned to Philadelphia where we remained Thursday, Friday and Saturday, the 24, 25 and 26th Nov. On Thursday my father held a meeting to explain the general principles of his system, which was well attended and where his sentiments were favorably received. On Friday he held a second meeting, where, in reply to a written application to do so, he expressed his opinion most distinctly that the Scriptures were no more inspired than any other book. This declaration was, to my surprise, generally applauded.

On Sunday 27 Nov. we set out at 3 oclock in the morning for Pittsburgh in the Stage, slept the first night at Harrisburg

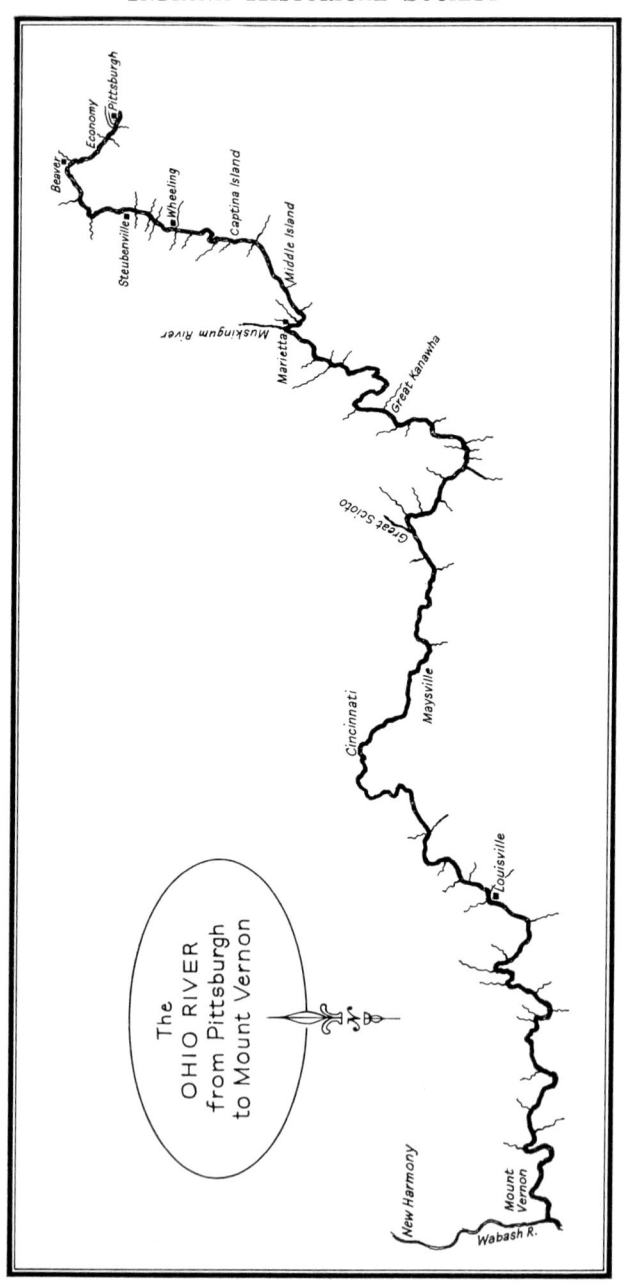

To Holland and To New Harmony

on the Susquehanna, the second night, Monday, at Chambersburg, the third Tuesday at Bedford, the fourth, Wednesday at Greensburg, and the fifth day we arrived at Pittsburg about three oclock..

All the inns on the road were excellent, except that at Greensburg, which was very bad. We met with great civility everywhere, had beautiful though rather cold weather, tolerably good roads, and stages, good horses, and on the whole an agreeable journey, the two first days through rather a level country and the others over the Alleganys consisting of several ridges, which present many beautiful and diversified views.

At Pittsburgh we staid from Thursday the 1st Decr till Thursday the 8th Decr. The three latter days were taken up in preparing and fitting out a keel boat to take us down the river: for we found that the river had not risen and that there was little chance for the steamboats to get down for some time to come. This keel boat was 85 feet long and 14 broad, with 6 large oars or sweeps. We divided into a ladies cabin or kitchen, a large cabin for dining etc; a small cabin for stores etc, where Mr. Maclure and I slept in two hammocks; and the forecastle for the boatmen, consisting of 11 persons. Our party consisted of Madame Fretageot, Mrs. Price, Mrs. Fisher, Lucy Sisterre, Sarah Turner,[113] Frances and Sarah Sisterre, Mr. Phiquepal and 10 of his scholars,[114] Messrs. Maclure, Say, LeSeuer, Price, Owen; RD Owen, Schmidt,[115] Balthazar,[116] Du Palais[117] and several workmen going to Harmony.[118]

Thursday 8th Decr.

Set out about 2 oclock and made 11 miles. Everything in considerable confusion. At night we saw a fire on the opposite side of the river, and Dr. Price, Say and myself got into the small boat, crossed over to them and found that it was made by the crew of a vessel which had just come up the river and who told us it was tolerably free from ice lower down. We went on to a log cabin which they told us was close at hand to get

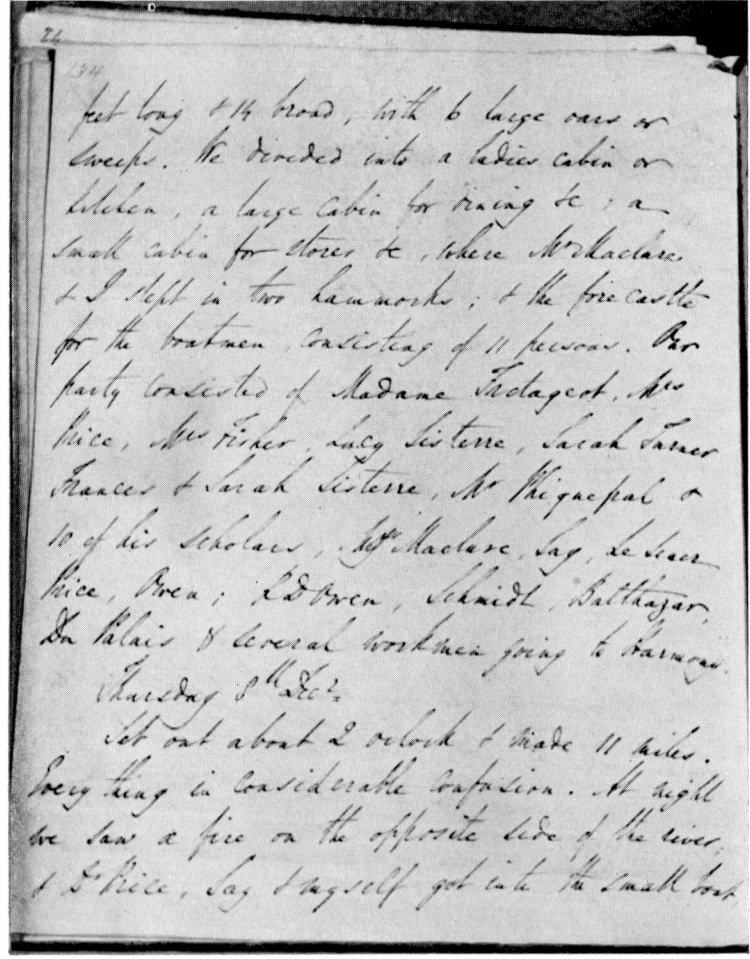

Page 134 of the Journal describing the "Philanthropist" and listing the Passengers

some milk—Finding they had but little we went on to another, where we found a good supply. These cabins were both situated on an island in the Ohio, about 7 miles long, the title to the property on which we were told, are very doubtful. These were the first log cabins I had ever entered and they

TO HOLLAND AND TO NEW HARMONY

appeared to me pretty comfortable. In one of them we found a negro family, jovial merry people, with whom we had a deal of fun. Altogether I like this first start very well.

Friday 9th Decr.

Set out abt seven and after making about 9 miles, we got aground, either on account of a strong sidewind or of the awkwardness of our pilot, on Merriman's riffle, a small and narrow rapid. Here, notwithstanding all the efforts of our men who got into the water several times, we remained aground all day. After breakfast, my father, Maclure, Phiquepal and Le Seur set out by land for Economy,[119] distant about 7 miles, whence he sent to our assistance 6 of the colonists with poles. They arrived about 6 oclock; and after great exertion for about an hour they got us off and we proceeded 2 miles further and then anchored for the night—The Harmonites remained over night with us: they appear to understand admirably how to act in concert, to be steady, retired, cautious and industrious, but not to possess superior intelligence or liberality of sentiment.—Some of our own people expressed great discontent at being obliged to work in the water which was then nearly at the freezing point; and one of them had an attack of cramp in the stomach after getting out. However, on the whole they stood it pretty well. Einige der Damen unserer Partei scheinen schon ganz ungedultig und unzufrieden, umso mehr da sie fast gar Nichts fuer sich thun koennen. Die anderen halten sich gut. [Some of the ladies of our party appear already quite impatient and dissatisfied the more so since they almost can't do anything for themselves. The others are holding up very well.]

Saturday 10th Decr.

Proceeded down to Economy, where we arrived about 9 oclock. Went on shore and saw Old Mr. Rapp[120] Frederick Rapp,[121] Gertrude Rapp,[122] and many of the Economists. Rapp's

Pittsburgh Waterfront with "Philanthropist" in Foreground
December 8, 1825. *C. A. Lesueur*

house is a very comfortable one; so is the inn, which is spacious and seems well kept. The colony appears very flourishing but I had little time to examine any part of it. Many of the Economists recollected William[123] and spoke with gt interest of him. They all welcomed us most cordially, and I judge them notwithstanding their staid demeanour to be a warmhearted set of people. I spoke with one of them this morning, while rowing at the same sweep with him for nearly an hour, and he gave me many details respecting Harmony. They have some fine deer and a couple of Elk at Economy in a fenced field. At Rapps we tasted some excellent wine made at Harmony, the best from wild grapes, which when kept several years improves remarkably.—My father left us here to proceed again to Pittsburgh to procure some deeds regarding the Harmony property, and we went on about 14 miles through a good deal of ice, which at one place was so thick as nearly to stop us altogether. Mme F. read aloud to us part of Fourier's[124] work in the evening: it is a strange and most original production, containing many excellent ideas, but mixed up with much which is,

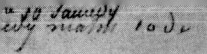

Economy, Pennsylvania
December 10, 1825. *C. A. Lesueur*

I think not practical. Ich finde dass diese Lebensart mir gut bekommt. Ich bin der Waerme, der Kaelte und sonst, den Muehesahlen viel mehr ausgesetzt wie sonst, aber ich bin wahrlich jetzt schon staerker und wuechtiger. Ich glaube ich koennte keine bessere Vor erziehung haben fuer Harmonie. Und es wird wol schon so den Anderen gehen. [I find that this way of life becomes me well. I am exposed to heat, cold, and also the hardships much more than otherwise, but I am truly already stronger and more vigorous. I believe I could not have a better preparation for Harmony and it will probably also be that way with the others.]

Sunday 11 Decr. 1825

Proceeded slowly along much impeded by ice till breakfast time. While at breakfast we were all called on deck to assist in getting through it. But as we found it gradually increasing in thickness and cut through with gt labor and difficulty, it became necessary to make for the shore and to lie by to wait for more favorable weather, particularly as we learnt that ahead of us waggons and horses were crossing the river. Dieses schien die wenig uebrige Geduld einiger unserer Damen ibnen ganz zu entnehmen. Sie beklagten oeffentlich ueber ihr ungluecklisches loos ud wollten mir nicht glauben, da ich ihnen sagte ich befinde mich ganz wohl ud fuende die Reise ueberhaupt sehr lustig. Ich fuerchte sie werden zurueck kehren ud das waere Schade. [This seemed to completely exhaust what little patience some of our ladies had left. They complained publicly about their unhappy lot and did not want to believe me when I told them that I felt quite well and found the journey above all quite amusing. I feared they might turn back and that would be a pity.] Went out a shooting with the rifle I had purchased at Pittsburgh. Saw several partridges but could not find any squirrels and killed nothing—The appearance of the woods is wild and magnificent in the extreme, immense trees lying across one another, and everything, apparently, in a perfect state of nature. The people seem civil and obliging, though they were rather scandalized at our hunting on Sunday. Read Fourier again. Wrote journal. Wrote to my father to Wheeling to inform him of our situation — There was a little snow today, the weather pretty cold.

Monday 12 Decr. 1825

After breakfast went out with Dr. Price, taking our rifles with us, to go along the river as far up as to Beaver, the county town, about 8 miles from our station, which is called "Safe Harbour." In going through the woods we saw a quantity of partridges and woodpeckers, a woodcock, doves etc, but no squirrels. We shot at many of the birds, but, as was to be expected, without effect. We found Beaver a small, scattered town containing 3 to 400 inhabitants, several good stores, where we purchased a few articles which we required; and returned about ½ past 6 to our boat. We found that, in our absence, two of M. Phiquepal's boys had fallen through the

Arrival of "Philanthropist" at Safe Harbor
December 11, 1825. C. A. Lesueur

ice into the water; and that too, in the middle of the river; but being able to swim, they got out again, though no assistance was near. M. Phiquepal himself, in getting over a fence fell with his head against a log and was so ill in consequence, that it became necessary to convey him to the nearest farmhouse and to leave him there. He and Mr. Lesuer had gone out shooting intendg to proceed to Georgetown, 4 miles down the river, when this accident happened. The day cold, and now and then snow. Die Damen werden noch immer verdriesslicher; besonders S. T. die heute morgen weinte waehrend des Fruehstueck. Es ist eigentl[ich] eine gute Erziehung fuer sie ud fuer uns alle. Ich fuer mich habe mich selten besser amuesiert. [The ladies are becoming evermore disgusted, particularly S. T. who cried this morning during breakfast. It is somewhat of a good education for her and for all of us. As for myself, seldom have I had a better time.]

Tuesday 13 Decr 1825.

Went out before breakfast to look for squirrels, but found none. After breakfast walked over to see M. Phiquepal, who had passed the night in a log cabin at about 2 miles from our boat. He was rather better. M. Lesuer who was with him, sketched the whole family as they sat at night engaged in their various occupations. M. Phiquepal was removed in a hammock to a cottage close to our boat where he was comfortably accommodated. We shot a squirrel, a partridge and a couple of doves. We afterwards went out in the evening about dusk and shot a couple of pheasants, as they sat on the trees. They are generally to be found on the trees early in the morning and late in the evening along the shores of the small runs, frequently sitting on ironwood trees. I made today an excellent shot with my rifle at a woodpecker, shooting off his head, but just afterwards when we had a regular squirrel hunt I missed him two or three times. Den Damen geht es etwas besser. [The ladies are somewhat better.] We had a consultation this evening as to what was to be done in our present situation, but he [we?] cd decide upon nothing till Mr. Schmidt returns from Wheeling or till we hear from my father. I fear the journey by land wd be too fatiguing for the ladies: and yet to remain here all winter appears to be great loss of time.—

Wednesday 14 Decr 1825.

Mr. Phiquepal was a good deal worse this morning, much fever and pain; Dr. Price bled him and about two o'clock he felt relieved: but it was not till then that we considered him out of danger. Had my rifle adjusted today by a Mr. Rice who seems an old hand, and who says it is a firstrate gun: he likewise showed me how to load it, clean it etc. Went out shooting in the afternoon, but found nothing. Played at Whist and read Fourier in the evening. It is much milder today, the sun pretty powerful; and some simptoms of a thaw. Den damen geht es viel besser. [The ladies are much better.] We have heard nothing from my father yet. From what I see of the people here, I think them an honest hospitable and sober race of men. Mr. Rice wd take nothing for adjusting my rifle today; and they scarcely appear to wish to take pecuniary advantage of anyone.—

Thursday 15 Decr. 1825.

Mr. Phiquepal a good deal better today. Went to Mr. Rice's and practised rifle shooting with tolerable success. Returned and called at a shoemaker's where I found an old man just dying: went to call the doctor, but before I returned he was dead. In the evening Schmidt arrived from Wheeling, where he had seen my father: Mr. Launes[125] accompanied him bringing with him a carriage to transport the ladies and anyone else who might wish to leave. This intelligence gave great satisfaction to some of our ladies, who were beginning to be sadly tired of their present situation. We concluded however upon nothing, determining to wait quietly Mr. Laune's arrival tomorrow.

Friday 16 Decr 1825.

Mr. Phiquepal passed a restless night and was a good deal worse this morning. During part of the night he had been delirious; and we were seriously alarmed about him. Towards evening, however he became more tranquil and better. Mr. Launes arrived about 10 oclock and there was much deliberating as to what was to be done. The weather is quite changed today: mild and continued rain, so as to afford us a prospect of getting off before long. Dr. Price, besides, cannot leave Mr. Phiquepal; and Mrs. P. does not wish to leave her husband. No one, therefore, except Mrs. Fisher, seemed inclined to go with Mr. Launes; and she accordingly set out with him to go to Yellow Springs.[126] On account of the rain no one went out.

Unidentified Passengers aboard "Philanthropist." *C. A. Lesueur*

I arrived [arranged?] various household matters, made balls for my rifle etc. In the evening we read Fourier: and afterwards had a long argument about the proper means of arranging matters at Harmony, about a costume[127] etc. Alles scheint jetzt viel besser zu gehen: Alle scheinen so zieml[ich] zufrieden: ud ich bin ueberzeugt, dass sie keine bessere Erziehung haetten haben koenen. Jetzt woerden sie in Harmonie zufrieden sein ud nuetzl[iche] Mitglieder werden. Sonst haetten sie es dort wol unbequem gefunden ud haetten auch Nichts fuer sich thun koennen. Die Frau F ist wahr[lich] ein ausgezeichnetes Weib in jeder Hinsicht. Die Art wie sie den Herrn P. heute bei seiner Krankheit handelte war mir ein starker Beweis ihrer Geistestaerke ud ihrer Vernunft. Der Herr M. scheint mir etwas eigensinnig ud heftig zu weilen aufzutreten. Herr S. den wir als Kapitaen ernannten geht

To Holland and To New Harmony

vertraut dazu, ud geht mit den Schiffsleuten auf die allerkluegste Weise um. [Everything seems now to go much better. All appear fairly satisfied and I am convinced that they could not have had a better preparation. Now they would be satisfied in Harmony and become useful members. Otherwise they would have found it inconvenient and would not have been able to do anything for themselves. Mme F is an excellent woman in every respect. The manner in which she acted today for Mr. P in his illness was for me a strong indication of her intelligence and her good sense.

Mr. M [Maclure] seems to me at times to act somewhat stubbornly and vehemently. Mr. S. [Say] whom we named captain goes about it competently and handles the crew in the most clever manner.

We have now agreed to have only two meals a day, viz one about 10 and the other about 5 oclock and find it an excellent regulation: it saves time and trouble and we find no inconvenience from it. We now begin to find out how to economize, so as to save labor as much as is consistent with convenience and comfort.

Saturday 17 Decr..

Went to see Mr. Phiquepal and found him a good deal better, though still restless. Hatte ein sonderbares Gespraech mit der Frau F. ueber unsere Familienverhaeltnisse. [Today I had a curious conversation with Mrs. F. about our family affairs.] Went out to look for squirrels, but finding none, fired at a mark, with pretty good success. In the evening read Fourier, and got into a conversation with Mr. Maclure regarding Hofwyl and with Madame regarding mathematics. The weather, damp with occasional rain and a little snow and rain mixed in the evening. Mr. Say spoke to the men about their dismissal, but as there appeared to be every chance of the weather breakg up almost immediately, they preferred accepting the offer we made them to remain for a few days without

"Philanthropist" Icebound at Safe Harbor
December 30, 1825. C. A. Lesueur

wages for their board only. Frances Sisterre is very unwell today; the rest in pretty good health.

Sunday 18 Decr 1825.

Mr. Phiquepal recovering. Not very cold; but snow all day: in the evening it cleared up to frost, the snow being then about 6 inches deep. Remained at home and at Mr. Phiquepals all day, engaged in domestic matters and in conversation. Read Fourier in the evening, on the management of infants, which subject he appears to me to treat in a masterly manner.

Monday 19 Decr 1825.

Out shooting, but killed nothing but a pheasant, though we had a small dog with us to start the birds. I sat up all night in Mr. Phiquepal's room who is now much better. Clear frost and deep snow.

To Holland and To New Harmony

Tuesday 20 Decr 1825.

The greater part of our crew were dismissed this morning, as there is no appearance of thaw and they are now useless to us. We retained only 3, besides two men who were going to Harmony. Es scheint mir dass Herr M. Alles auf viel zu verdaechtige Weise ansieht, ud gewand dadurch sich zuweilen Schwierigkeiten thun macht. [It seems to me that Mr. M. looks at everything in a much too suspicious manner and manages thereby at times to make difficulties for himself.] As we had not any note of each mans agreement, we were obliged to trust to what they told us, and to pay them accordingly.

Shot at a mark and went after pheasants in the evening, but though I had an excellent chance, I missed three shots and came home without anything. Clear frost and a little snow in the middle of the day. Read a little of Fourier and conversed on various subjects in the evening.

Wednesday 21 Decr 1825.

After breakfast heard that John Harrison, one of our neighbors was going out with a dog to shoot pheasants: determined to go with him, but on going to his house, found he had gone half an hour since: followed him without being able to meet him; but on my return, I came up to him just as he shot for the second time at a deer—This shot killed it. It was a fine year old buck and the first deer I had ever seen killed. Returned to John Rice, and learned various things relating to the management of a rifle, for instance how to case harden the skrew nails, which is done in this way. Burn some scraps of leather and pound them when burnt; scrape and burn some scraps of horn and add to these a little soot along with some salt. Put the whole into a small earthen vessel over the fire and put the nails into it. Cover it up with bits of wood and set fire to them. Let it stand 20 minutes. Then throw them

Cutting through Ice to the Open Channel, Safe Harbor
January 8, 1826. C. A. Lesueur

into cold water. Afterwards polish the heads a little by rubbing them on a bit of wood—I learnt too that deer oil is the best for the locks of guns; and mutton suet the best for greasing the patches; that the barrel after shooting should be carefully washed out with boiling water, the lock taken out and carefully cleaned and a little oil rubbed over it: that the barrel shd be oiled before laying it by, particularly in cold weather. Clear frost still.

Thursday 22 Decr 1825.

Went with John Rice to a shooting match in this neighbourhood. We shot a pheasant on way. Found it about 6 miles, heavy walking through the woods admidst deep snow. Found about a dozen persons assembled, who shot for various articles. I gained a pocket handkerchief and J. Rice gained a turkey and a pair of braces. We had a most fatiguing walk home in the dark carrying the turkey we had won and our rifles. We sat down three several times in the midst of the snow,

TO HOLLAND AND TO NEW HARMONY

and when I arrived at the boat, I was more fatigued than, I believe, I ever was in the course of my life. Indeed I was so sick with fatigue that I could not eat a morsel. The shootg was conducted with tolerable temper; but the persons present seemed to me in low spirits, without any appearance of mirth or fun.

Friday 23d Decr 1825.

Today Mr. Maclure, who has had a bad cold, set out for Beaver, and Madame F. accompanied him. I went to John Rice's and shot a little. Turkey oil and fat are excellent for guns. Hiccory is the best wood for ramrods. After dinner went out with the ladies on the ice and had some good fun. Played at cards afterwards. Clear, cold weather.

Saturday 24th Decr 1825.

Went out to look for deer, but found none. Shot a little at a target. Staid some time with Mr. Phiquepal. A little rain and mild weather: appearance of thaw, the river falling. The friendlyness of the inhabitants here is very remarkable. Whenever you pass by their doors you are asked to walk in and welcomed with unfeigned pleasure.-

Sunday 25th Decr 1825.

Christmas day. This morng we found on getting up that it had been raining all night, and the snow was fast disappearing. The rain continued till abt 2 o'clock, when it cleared up to frost and thus destroyed our hopes of gettg away, which had been excited by the change of weather. After breakfast visited M. Phiquepal, and had a good deal of conversation with him, principally as to the meang of various words, and as to the best articles for the Harmony Gazette. After dinner went to see him again with Say, who related various anecdotes of Indians, showing their perfect composure in cases of danger or of sudden alarm or of extreme pain, the tenacity with which they

"Philanthropist" tied up at Steubenville beside a Ferry
January 9, 1825. C. A. Lesueur

nourish revenge etc.—I believe the evils of the savage and of the civilized state are nearly balanced—They have many excellent qualities, which we most irrationally neglect to cultivate, but they fail to attain much of which we are in possession.

Monday 26 Dec 1825.

Out shooting: killed a pheasant. Hard frost. Mr. Phiquepal still recovering. A long conversation at night on various subjects, of costume etc. Sad complaints from the evening police.

Tuesday 27 Decr. 1825.

Out shooting without success. Frost, but not very severe.

Wednesday 28 Decr 1825.

After breakfast set out for Beaver, where I found Mr. Maclure and Madame. Went to the mill at 2½ miles distance on the Big Beaver Creek, and purchased 3 bushels of wheat. The weather mild. Had a long conversation in the evening with a methodist clergyman on religion and politics. He reasoned with qt good temper and some talent, but has the most incorrect ideas. It is extremely difficult by abstract reasoning to convince even of the plainest truths one, whose mind has been for years trained by ingenious and self believed sophistry to support irrational ideas. The vagueness of the terms generally used greatly increases this difficulty; for instance "free agent" "liberty of choice" "mere machine" "responsible being" etc. etc.

Thursday 29 Decr 1825.

At Beaver. Wrote to my mother, and to Joseph Applegath. Determined to proceed next day to Pittsburgh to obtain money and other necessaries. Hatte ein langes Gespraech mit der Frau F. ueber meine Verhaeltnisse zu hause. [Had a long conversation with Mme F. about my situation at home.] From a description of Parisian manners which Madame gave me this evening, I am induced to think that many parts of them are most worthy of imitation amongst ourselves; for instance the perfect freedom from restraint or ceremony which characterizes their intercourse with one another. And their disposition to make the best of every situation and enjoy without excess the present moment: then again their civility even to perfect strangers and their easy politeness to one another. Mild and some snow.

Friday 30 Decr 1825.

Had a wet uncomfortable walk through the rain to the boat, having determined to return thither in consequence of the thaw. This thaw has at length broken up the ice, so that on my arrival at the boat I found the river open; and heard that the precedg night the party had been disturbed by a noise resembling peals of thunder in consequence of the ice breakg up; that they had immediately sprung from their beds and

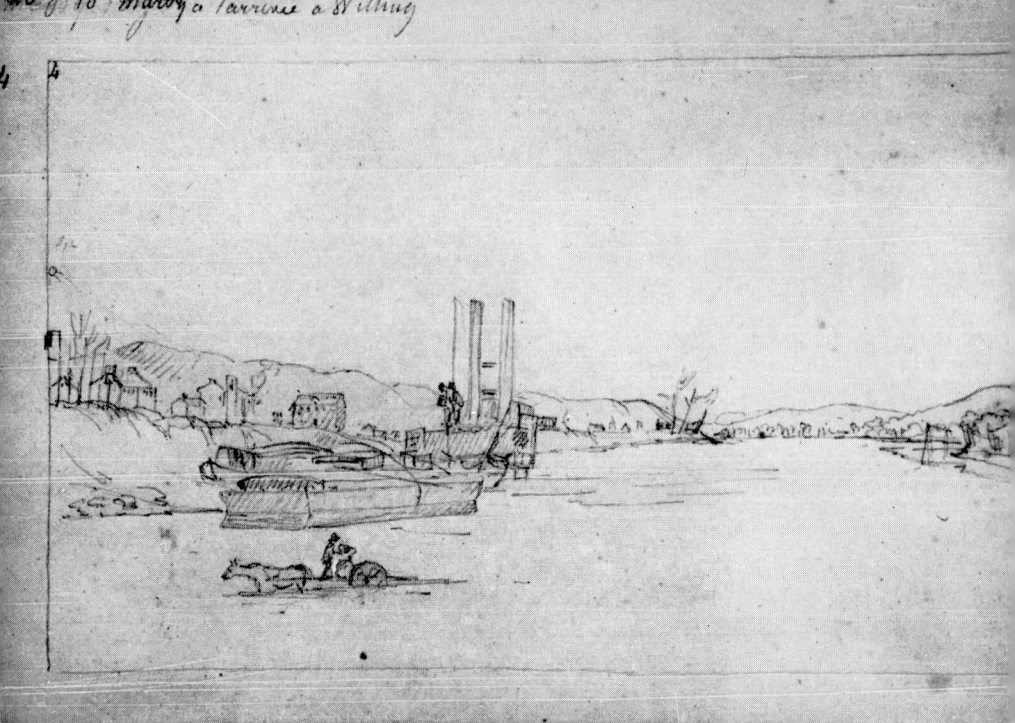

Waterfront at Wheeling, with two Keelboats and Steamboat Beyond January 10, 1826. C. A. Lesueur

secured most of the baggage on shore. However after some alarm and much amusement they concluded when the ice appeared to have past to return quietly to the boat which they did, putting their trunks all on board again. I regretted having lost this scene, which they say afforded infinite amusement to all concerned. Still mild and rainy with a little snow.

Saturday 31 Decr 1825.

Rather mild, but no rain. Went to John Rice's to have my rifle adjusted. Found that it shot a little to the left and had the sights altered a little. When a rifle shoots to the right or left, the *front* sight must be altered *to* the side the bullets fall, and the hind sight *from* that side.

Mr. Maclure and Madame arrived from Beaver; but as the ice from up the river had not yet come down it was thought advisable not to set out yet. We held a long consultation on the subject in the evening, in which there was great variety of opinions, Dr. Price urging setting off immediately in the morning and most of the others being of opinion that it wd be more prudent to wait a day or two here and let the rest of the ice pass down first.

Jany. 1st 1826. Sunday.

The new year was ushered in under very bleak auspices. A high, cold wind blowing up the river, with snow and sleet. Very little ice passing down. Read Fourier, went to Mr. Phiquepal's, cast bullets etc.

Jany. 2d 1826 Monday.

Snow and sleet. After breakfast copied a little drawing of Mr. Lesuer's to send home. Dr. Price discovered a deer on the ice and we went out immediately after it. But the ice was too weak to bear us, and the deer too far off to enable us to shoot it. In the meantime another deer crossed: immediately after it came out of the water I fired at it without effect. It recrossed passing down opposite our keelboat and was shot on the other side. In the evening read Fourier, drew a little, assisted in making some bread etc.

Tuesday Jany. 3, 1826.

Out shooting and tracking deer all day. Followed one deer track 3 or 4 miles, until, as it was getting late I gave up the chase as hopeless. The deer was wounded by another man about quarter of an hour afterwards on the same spot where I tracked it to. Not very cold.

Wednesday Jany. 4.

Wrote a dft on Saml Spackman for $200 which I gave Mr. Maclure who with Madame set off for Stubenville today. The weather clear and rather cold. Practiced shooting at a mark. Afterwards shot with my rifle a pheasant and a pigeon.

Thursday Jany. 5.

Out deer hunting. Saw a deer shot within 60 yards of me by a young man, Ephraim Spencer, who had seen it cross a

"Philanthropist" approaching Captina Island
January 10, 1826. C. A. Lesueur

field close to his cabin. Shot a little at a target. Clear frost and very cold. Mr. Maclure and Madame set out for Stubenville.

Friday Jan. 6.

Out hunting deer. Saw a fine buck which started about 120 yards before me, but so that I cd not get a shot at it. Dr. Price who was out with me saw 3 deer which he tracked till it became dark. The best plan in deerhunting appears to be to walk on slowly and cautiously, stopping every little while to listen and look all round. Clear but not very cold. We hear that Whitwell and McDonald are at Economy and hope to see them soon.

Saturday Jany. 7.

Went out in the morning to look for pheasants, but it became so wet, that I returned to John Rice's and practiced shootg there. In the evening Virginia Dupalais[128] arrived from Beaver whither her brother and Lesuer had gone to meet her.

To Holland and To New Harmony

They informed us that McDonald and Whitwell were at Beaver, but did not come on on account of the rain. However about 7 o'clock they arrived. Great was their astonishment at all they saw and heard, so that they wd scarcely believe we had lived comfortably in such a situation for a month past. They had been well received by the President who seemed interested in inspecting the model.[129] They had passed about a week at Economy and only heard by chance of our being at Safe Harbour.

Sunday Jany. 8.

Macdonalds and Whitwells astonishment did not seem to abate today on seeing how they were received and addressed. The former did not seem above half pleased with it: he wished for a little more ceremony, I believe.

We determined to cut through the ice about 150 yds to the open channel. This we effected in the course of the day, then laid in a stock of provisions, wood etc. got Mr. Phiquepal on board and prepared everything for startg.

Die Dame die gestern ankahm scheint ganz ud gar sich unserer Lebensweise fuegen zu wollen ud haelt sich wirkl[ich] recht brav. [The lady who arrived yesterday seems to want to fit entirely into our way of life and conducts herself really quite bravely.]

Dr. Price fell into the river through the ice up to his neck, but got out without other inconvenience than a good wetting.

Had a long discussion in the evening with Macdonald about expediency of *varying* employments on which subjects we widely disagreed. It appears to me the greatest mistake to suppose it rational to make men mere producing machines and to treat them as such, and to estimate their happiness by the quantity of their productions. We must be careful, too, not to forget that happiness is the object of our pursuit; and that we succeed, not in proportion to the extent of our surplus

"Philanthropist" with Middle Island in Background
January 11, 1826. *C. A. Lesueur*

Waterfront at Cincinnati with Three Steamboats and a Keelboat
January 17, 1826. *C. A. Lesueur*

To Holland and To New Harmony

productions, but in proportion to the measure of happiness which the members of the society enjoy. Rather mild and damp weather.

Monday Jany. 9.

Mild and fine weather. Took leave of Safe Harbour after havg been detained there for 4 weeks and a few hours. We found the river tolerably clear as we went down. We had all hands on deck, even the ladies, assisting in rowing and got on very well. The scenery very similar to that in the neighbourhood of Safe Harbour; wooded hills cleared here and there and occasionally a village or a small town laid out. We rowed all day and arrived at Stübenville about 5 oclock. There we staid for a few minutes, during which time Judge Tappan[130] of that place came on board and told us that he wished to send his son along with us to Harmony to be educated. He accordingly sent him on board and we drifted down the river all night. Next morning (made abt 40 miles today)

Tuesday Jany 10.

We found ourselves at 8 oclock at Wheeling. There we staid three hours. Found Madame and Maclure there and took them on board. We purchased various articles of which we stood in need, and then pushed off. Fine mild weather. Up on deck rowing the greater part of the day. We made today about 40 miles more. Drifted all night. Today one of the boys, little Victor,[131] fell into the water, while dipping a mug for water: William McCarter[132] jumped in immediately, and succeeded in rescuing him.

Wednesday Jany 11.

A strong head wind which prevented us from making more than 10 or 12 miles till about 5 oclock, when we put on shore abt 15 miles above Marietta. On going on shore, we were surprised to find signs of civilization such as are seldom to be

met with, and on proceeding a little further to enter a remarkably neat two story brickhouse. The inhabitants who appeared to be of a superior class to any we had seen on the river welcomed us most heartily, and afterwards came down to our boat to see us there. Their names were Dana and they appeared to know all about my father and to be much interested in the experiment of Harmony. We drifted down at night arrived at Marietta abt 12 oclock, when a few of our party went on shore to purchase bread etc. Next morning
(Fine mild weather)

Thursday Jany 12.

About 4 oclock in consequence of a misunderstanding on the part of the watch, who mistook one island for another, we got aground at the head of an island and remained there about an hour and a half, when, the water rising, we got off. Beautiful weather, with a little frost in the morning. Went on shore for milk and had a long row after the boat to reach it again. Made about 95 miles in 24 hours from the time of our getting off. Fine mild weather. In the evening several remained on deck till quite late, singing, dancing etc.

Friday Jany 13.

Fine weather. Continued to make way at a good rate, as the river is gradually and rapidly rising. Various discussions, metaphysical etc. in the evening.

Saturday Jany 14.

Continued to make good way, till towards evening when we arrived at Maysville; and there two of our hands left us, and we took a man on board, who wishes to go to Harmony. After passing Maysville the wind rose ahead of us and we made but little way. In the evening it became much colder.

Wharf at Mount Vernon, Indiana
January 23, 1826. *C. A. Lesueur*

"Philanthropist" flying a Streamer bearing name "Harmony"
January 24, 1826. *C. A. Lesueur*

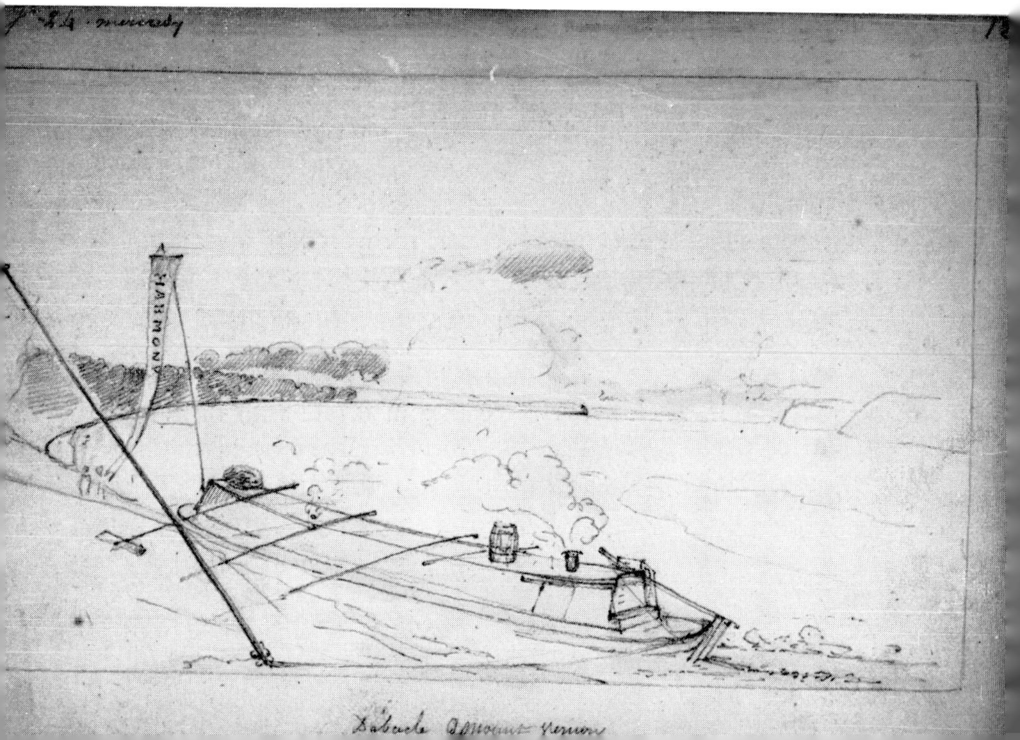

Sunday Jany 15.

Extremely strong head wind with very cold weather, thermometer at 22°. Made but little way and stopped toward evening. Had some long discussions with one another on various subjects. Der McD. scheint viele falsche Ideen zu besitzen, ud sich die Sachen ganz anders vorzustellen als wir anderen. [McDonald seems to possess many false ideas and to imagine things quite differently from the rest of us.]

Monday Jany 16.

Still cold and wind ahead. Found the ice coming down and were completely surrounded with it all day, so that we could not row, but floated down with it. About 6 oclock we reached Cincinnati, and got in with considerable difficulty through the ice. Called on Mr. Clark my father's agent, and found that my father had left this abt a week since.

Tuesday Jany 17.

At Cincinnati, which is by far the most regular and chearful lookg town we have seen in the west. Saw several of my fathers friends there. Went with Say to purchase various articles. Saw the museum of Nat. History, small; but apparently well arranged. In the evening heard Captn. Symes lecture on his new theory of the earth. His theory appears plausible, and the great collection of facts which he brings to bear upon it evinces his industry and I think considerable talent and penetration. The matter appears to me worthy of investigation, as the subject of an expedition.[133]

Wednesday Jany 18.

Set out at 8 oclock from Cincinnati and proceeded about 63 miles by 11 at night. Weather moderate with little wind. Read the Apocryphical Testament which appears to me a curious and instructive document.

New Harmony from a nearby Hill
Undated. *C. A. Lesueur*

Thursday Jany 19.

Weather moderate. In the morning found ourselves about 40 miles from Louisville. Nach dem Morgen essen [?] gab es ein haeftiges Gespraech ueber dem was geschehen war in Hinsicht unseres frueheren Gespraechs. Ich weis wirkl[ich] nicht wo dieses hinaus will: es wird aber wohl nuetzlich sein. [After the morning meal there was a lively conversation about what had happened with reference to our previous conversation. I really don't know how this is going to end: however it will be useful.] In the evening we arrived at Louisville. Went to see Mr. Stewart, and visited with him one of the reading rooms, where we found accidentally Joseph Neef.[134]

Friday Jany 20.

Floated down the river rapidly. On deck rowing a great part of the day. Floated all night.

Saturday Jany 21 & Sunday Jany 22.

Continued to proceed down the river, though slowly; being much detained by contrary winds, which obliged to land on the Indiana shore, where I saw canebrake for the first time, and nearly got lost in it.

Monday Jany 23.

Arrived about 9 oclock at Mount Vernon, where we found Schmidt in waiting for us. I set out immediately on horse back for Harmony, where I arrived about 4 oclock. Found that Wm had gone to meet me and had taken another road, so that we missed one another. Arrived just in time to hear my father address the inhabitants.

APPENDIX

PASSENGERS ON BOARD THE "PHILANTHROPIST"

As is clearly indicated in the following lists the reports of the four persons who have left a record of who were passengers on the "Philanthropist" are far from being in agreement. In part the discrepancies may have occurred because several of those who went on board at Pittsburgh left the boat before the journey ended, while others came on at points along the river. Also the dismissal of some of the crew during the long delay at Safe Harbor because of ice probably accounts for some of the variation in numbers. In any case, these lists are of interest independent of their completeness.

Passengers recorded by Robert Dale Owen in his journal:[1]

	Men	Children	Women
Mme Fretageot			1
Mrs. Price			1
Mrs. Fisher			1
Lucy Sisterre			1
Sarah Turner			1
Frances Sisterre			1
Sarah Sisterre			1
Phiquepal and 10 students	1	10	
Maclure	1		
Say	1		
LeSueur	1		
Price	1		
Owen	1		
R. D. Owen	1		
Schmidt	1		
Balthazar	1		
DuPalais	1		
Virginia DuPalais (boarded Jan. 7)			1
Macdonald (boarded Jan. 7)	1		

Indiana Historical Society

Stedman Whitwell (boarded Jan. 7)	1		
Son of Judge Tappan (boarded Jan. 9)		1	
Several workmen	?		
11 boatmen	11		
Total	23	11	8

Passengers recorded by Donald Macdonald:[2]

	Men	Children	Women
Robert Dale Owen	1		
Dr. and Mrs. Price and 3 children	1	3	1
Miss Sistair and two sisters			3
Mr. Dupalais and his sister	1		1
Miss Turner			1
Mr. Le Seur and one child	1	1	
Mr. Phiquepal and 10 boys	1	10	
Mr. Smith [Schmidt]	1		
Mr. Say	1		
Beal, a carpenter, and wife and child	1	1	1
Mr. Maclure	1		
Mme Fretageot			1
Mr. Stedwell (boarded Jan. 7)	1		
Macdonald himself (boarded Jan. 7)	1		
Son of Judge Tappan (boarded Jan. 9)		1	
6 boatmen and captain	7		
Total	18	16	8

Passengers recorded by Victor Colin Duclos:[3]

	Men	Children	Women
Mme Fretageot			1
A. E. Fretageot		1	
Allan Ward		1	
Mark Penrose		1	
Phiquepal d'Arusmont	1		
Charles A. Lesueur, artist and naturalist	1		
Thomas Say, naturalist	1		
M. Chase, chemist	1		
Mrs. Chase, artist and musician			1
Cornelius Tiebout, artist and engraver	1		
Lucy Sistaire and two sisters			3
Virginia Dupalais and brother	1		1

To Holland and To New Harmony

John Beal, wife, and child Caroline	1	1	1
William Maclure	1		
Captain McDonald	1		
Balthazar, a Swiss	1		
Charles Falque ⎫			
Amedie Dufour ⎟ pupils			
Peter L. Duclos ⎬ of		5	
Victor C. Duclos ⎟ Phiquepal			
Miss Tiebout ⎭			
Speakman and family	1	?	1
Robert Dale Owen	1		
Gerard Troost, chemist and zoologist	1		
Robert Owen	1		
Total	14	9	8

Passengers recorded by Charles Alexandre Lesueur:[4]

"Le 27 Novembre 1825 un *quille-boat*, qui portait le beau nom de *Philanthropist*, s'éloignait de Pittsburg et descendait l'Ohio, avec 27 passagers et 10 hommes d'équipage."

	Men	Children	Women
William Maclure	1		
Robert Owen and son	2		
Thomas Say	1		
C. A. Lesueur	1		
Wm. Phiquepal	1		
Mme Fretageot			1
Price, his wife and 3 children	1	3	1
Smith [Schmidt]	1		
[Victor] Dupalais	1		
Bill [Beal?] and daughter	1	1	
Miss Hale [?]			1
5 women			5
6 children		6	
Total	10	10	8

Petty Journal 1, June 27, 1825—July 27, 1826, of the New Harmony Community, in the New Harmony Library of the Workingmen's Institute, carries charges entered at the tavern on January 28, 1826, by passengers from the "Philanthropist." The names are recorded as follows: William McClure, Thomas Say, Andre Phiquepal, Donald McDonald, Steadman Whitwell, Balthazar Abernasser, William McArthur, Robert D. Owen, John Beal, Charles Schmidt, Marie Louise Duclos Fretageot, Helen Fisher, Lucy Systerre, Virginia Dupalais, Wm. Herring, Andre Dupalais, and Charles Laseur.

NOTES

Introduction

[1] See note 24, below, pp. 272-73.

[2] *The New-Harmony Gazette*, November 15, 22, 29, December 6, 1826; January 17, 24, 1827. References to the trip to Holland are found in contributions by him in *The Free Enquirer* (New York), January 15 and November 12, 1831.

[3] Robert Dale Owen, *Threading My Way, Twenty-seven Years of Autobiography* (New York, G. W. Carleton & Co., 1874), pp. 267-68. At this time Owen could not recall whether William Maclure was aboard the "Philanthropist" or not. As a matter of fact, there are indications that this journal was not at hand when Robert Dale wrote his article, "The Social Experiment at New Harmony," for the August 1873 issue of the *Atlantic*. Here he states (p. 236), "whether William Maclure . . . accompanied us, or came on a few weeks later, I am not quite certain." Maclure is listed in the journal as one of the passengers. See below, p. 237.

[4] Richard W. Leopold, *Robert Dale Owen, A Biography* (Harvard University Press, 1940), p. 6.

[5] See Appendix below, pp. 265-66.

[6] For further biographical material on Robert Dale Owen see the work by Leopold cited above, note 4, and his own autobiographical writings, principally *Threading My Way*, and Elinor Pancoast and Anne E. Lincoln, *The Incorrigible Idealist: Robert Dale Owen in America* (Bloomington, Ind., Principia Press, 1940).

To Holland And To New Harmony

[1] The Owen residence situated on the Clyde River near New Lanark.

[2] This is probably the "Carl H——" described by Robert Dale Owen in *The Free Enquirer*, January 15, 1831, pp. 89-91. Entitled "Destiny," the article concerns a young man, a native of Holland, who seemed to have a premonition of his death. Owen wrote, "Ten years ago, Carl H—— was a school-fellow of mine. . . . I left school and lost sight of Carl, until a year or two afterwards, when I visited Holland and we met again." However, the above journal entry indicates that Higgins had been at Braxfield and later entries indicate that he accompanied Robert Dale to Holland. See note 33, below.

[3] Brother of the two phrenologists, Andrew and George Combe, Abram Combe (1785-1827) was a tanner, with a prosperous business in Edinburgh.

In 1820, on visiting New Lanark, he became a convert to Robert Owen's ideas, and devoted the remainder of his life and fortune to the promulgation of the principles of co-operation. Most significant of all his activities was the prominent role he played in the founding of the co-operative community of Orbiston, located on the banks of the Calder east of Glasgow, which was one of the largest, more progressive, and for the space of some two years reasonably successful experiments established by followers and associates of Robert Owen. For a fuller account of Combe's life and works and the Orbiston community see Frank Podmore, *Robert Owen. A Biography* (2 volumes. New York, D. Appleton and Company, 1907), II, 356-73, and George Jacob Holyoake, *The History of Co-operation in England: Its Literature and Its Advocates* (2 volumes. London, Trubner & Co., 1875), I, 271-77. The *New-Harmony Gazette* carried discussions of Combe's views and reviews of his books. See, for example, the issue of January 17, 1827, pp. 124-25.

4 Located in Lombard Street, this was the site of a chemical factory owned by the Quaker philanthropist William Allen and also apparently of his residence. See below, note 26.

5 The London Infant School Society was founded in 1824. It was an outgrowth of the infant school opened at Brewers' Green, Westminster, in 1819, under the direction of a committee headed by Lord Brougham (see note 11, below) who had visited New Lanark where he had been much impressed by the infant schools. The Westminster school was patterned after them. Podmore, *Robert Owen*, I, 150n-51n, 159-60.

6 A banker and member of Parliament, John Smith was a frequent visitor at New Lanark and was a member of the committee headed by Lord Brougham which founded the infant school in Westminster. *The Life of Robert Owen by Himself*, with an Introduction by M. Beer (New York, Alfred A. Knopf, 1920), p. 196.

7 James Morrison (1790-1857), successful merchant and political liberal who was interested in Robert Owen's New Lanark experiment. *Dictionary of National Biography* (22 volumes. Oxford University Press, 1959-60), XIII, 1005-06.

8 Perhaps John Minter Morgan (1782-1854), a writer of ample fortune who devoted himself to philanthropy. In 1819 he published *Remarks on the Practicability of Mr. Owen's Plan to Improve the Condition of the Lower Classes*, which was followed by other writings on education and religion. *Dictionary of National Biography*, XIII, 919-20. He is mentioned in *The Life of Robert Owen by Himself*, p. 292.

9 Probably Philip Orkney Skene, a promoter of and contributor to co-operative projects. After serving with distinction in the British Army abroad he entered the Middle Temple, became interested in Owen's New Lanark project, and thereafter devoted himself to promoting similar efforts. He died in 1837 at the age of forty-four. Philip O. Skene had a brother G. R. Skene, described as an able and influential man, who served as secre-

To Holland and To New Harmony

tary of the British Association for Promoting Co-operative Knowledge, organized in 1829. Holyoake, *The History of Co-operation in England,* I, 126, 353-54; II, 165.

[10] Edward Irving (1792-1834), Scottish clergyman of considerable magnetism who came to London in 1822 as minister at Hatton Garden Chapel, Holborn. He acquired much fame as a preacher but suffered as an easy prey to flatterers and fanatics. He was later (1833) charged with heresy. *Dictionary of National Biography,* X, 489-93. Leopold mentions Robert Dale listening "with delight to Edward Irving's frank discussion of matrimony." *Robert Dale Owen,* p. 17.

[11] Henry Peter Brougham (1778-1868) was one of the founders of and a contributor to the *Edinburgh Review* (1802) and a founder of the University of London (1828). He had a deep interest in the abolition of slavery and was a pioneer in the field of popular education. In 1816 he visited Hofwyl and returned with great enthusiasm for Fellenberg's use of industrial and agricultural instruction. The author of *Practical Observations upon the Education of the People* (1825), he founded mechanics institutes and the Society for the Diffusion of Useful Knowledge (1827-1844). He was chancellor under Lord Grey at the time of the passage of the Reform Bill. See note 5, above; *Dictionary of National Biography,* II, 1356-66, and *Encyclopaedia of the Social Sciences* (25 volumes. New York, Macmillan, 1930-35), III, 14.

[12] *Der Freischütz* (The Free-Shooter), an opera by Carl Maria von Weber with libretto by Friedrich Kind. Its first performance, in Berlin on July 18, 1821, was a triumph and its popularity in London was so great that it was presented simultaneously in three theaters. *Encyclopedia of the Opera,* compiled by David Ewen (New York, Hill and Wang, 1963), pp. 164-65.

[13] John Lepard (d. 1878 at age of eighty-seven) was a London bookseller. Frederic Boase, *Modern English Biography* (Rev. ed. London, Frank Cass, 1965).

[14] Perhaps Edward Cowper (1790-1852), inventor and teacher who was responsible for developing the method of printing paper on both sides at once and for improving the speed of printing. It has been said that he did for the printing machine what Watts did for the steam engine. Cowper served as professor of Manufacturing Art and Mechanics at King's College, London, where his success as a lecturer was attributed in large measure to his adoption of the Pestalozzian principles of instruction. His business partner and brother-in-law was Augustus Applegath (1788-1871), perhaps the brother of the Miss Applegath mentioned below. *Dictionary of National Biography,* IV, 1310; *The Gentleman's Magazine* (London), 1852, pt. 2, pp. 647-48.

[15] William Thompson (1785-1833), Irish landowner, student of Jeremy Bentham's utilitarianism, and an enthusiastic supporter of Owen's views on the co-operative system. In 1824 he published *An Inquiry into the Principles*

INDIANA HISTORICAL SOCIETY

of the Distribution of Wealth Most Conducive to Human Happiness, laying the foundation of scientific socialism, and in 1827 *Labour Rewarded,* which included practical directions for establishing co-operative communities. Holyoake, *The History of Co-operation in England,* I, 109-11.

[16] Organized in 1824, the London Co-operative Society sought to pave the way for the acceptance of Robert Owen's views of society by lectures, discussions, and publications. Podmore, *Robert Owen,* II, 374-76; Holyoake, *The History of Co-operation in England,* I, 113-14.

[17] Thomas Phillips (1770-1845), portrait painter, who was elected an associate of the Royal Academy in 1804 and professor of painting of the Academy in 1825. *Dictionary of National Biography,* XV, 1102-03.

[18] Mary Dale Stewart, sister of Robert Dale Owen's mother and wife of the Reverend James Haldane Stewart, an Evangelical clergyman of the Church of England. *The Life of Robert Owen by Himself,* p. 139.

[19] The building in the Strand planned by Sir William Chambers which dates from 1775 and is presently occupied by the Register-General's Office and other government offices. The rooms to the right of the Strand entrance were at one time used for the exhibition of pictures of the Royal Academy.

[20] Sir Thomas Lawrence (1769-1830), president of the Royal Academy and famous for his portraits of notable contemporaries. His "The Master Lambton," the likeness of Charles William Lambton, son of John George Lambton, 1st Earl of Durham and Governor General of Canada, is among his celebrated pictures of children. *Dictionary of National Biography,* XI, 719-26.

[21] James Henry Leigh Hunt (1784-1859), English poet, essayist, critic, and journalist. Politically a radical, he published articles attacking George IV in his paper *The Examiner,* which led to a two-year imprisonment, 1813-15. He had a strong influence on his contemporaries, especially the poets Byron, Shelley, and Keats. *Dictionary of National Biography,* X, 267-74.

[22] Joseph Foster, of Bromley, a member of the Society of Friends, was one of the six men in Robert Owen's new partnership formed at New Lanark to carry out his ideas of co-operation in 1813. The others were Jeremy Bentham, William Allen, John Walker, Joseph Fox, and Michael Gibbs. *Life of Robert Owen by Himself,* pp. 123, 131.

[23] One of Robert Owen's partners (see note 22, above), Gibbs, a member of the Church of England, was later Lord Mayor of London.

[24] A young girl of humble origin but possessed of extraordinary beauty and charm whom Robert Dale had first noticed while teaching in the New Lanark schools. He prevailed upon his sister Anne and then his parents to accept her into their household, where she lived as a member of the family from 1823 until about 1830. Though Margaret (or Jessie, as he calls her in his autobiographical writings) was just a child, Robert Dale fell deeply in love with her, with "a truer and tenderer affection . . . than, perhaps, I

TO HOLLAND AND TO NEW HARMONY

may ever chance to have for anyone again." Thus he wrote to his mother in a letter of August 12, 1830.

The purchase of Harmonie from the Harmonists appealed to Robert Dale not only for the social reform possibilities but also because, as he reports in *Threading My Way*, ". . . If our family settled in Western America, it would facilitate my marriage to Jessie." When he departed for the New World, Margaret was only thirteen, and he left without confessing his love. On his return visit to Braxfield in 1827, he found her "beautiful and interesting beyond my remembrance or expectation"—but still too young for marriage. A promise was made to his mother to wait another three years when Margaret would be eighteen. But before this time had elapsed Margaret was married to a young man of her own social station. Thirty years were to pass before they met again, and it was not until then that each confessed his early love for the other. *Threading My Way*, pp. 215-31, 241; Robert Dale Owen to his wife Mary Jane Robinson Owen, September 29, 1832, Branigin–Owen Collection, Library of the New Harmony Workingmen's Institute; George J. Holyoake, "Unpublished Correspondence of the Robert Owen Family," in *The Co-operative News and Journal of Associated Industry*, XXXV, No. 18 (April 30, 1904).

[25] Probably Cornelius Hanbury, son-in-law of William Allen of Plough Court. See note 26, below.

[26] Scientist, philanthropist, abolitionist, and Quaker, William Allen (1770-1843) was another of Robert Owen's new partners in the New Lanark mills in 1813 and took considerable interest in Owen's project. However, the latter found him bustling and ambitious and his mind too limited by Quaker prejudices. Stoke-Newington was the site of a school founded by William Allen. *The Life of Robert Owen by Himself*, pp. 131-32; *Life of William Allen, with Selections from His Correspondence* (2 volumes. Philadelphia, 1847).

[27] Perhaps John Gray of Galashiels, author and lecturer who was concerned with devising means of improving society. His published works included *A Lecture on Human Happiness* (London, 1825), to which was appended "The articles of agreement drawn up and recommended by the London Co-operative Society, for the formation of a community on the principles of mutual co-operation, within fifty miles of London"; *The New Social System: a Treatise on the Principle of Exchange* (Edinburgh, 1831); *The Currency Question* (Edinburgh, 1847); and *Lectures on the Nature and Use of Money* (Edinburgh, 1848).

[28] Thomas Barnes (1785-1841), editor of the *Times* from 1817 to 1841.

[29] The reference is probably to Owen's lectures in the United States House of Representatives before the President, members of Congress, and others, on February 25 and March 7, 1825. They were published in London in 1825 under the title *Owen's American Discourses*.

[30] The town house of John Walker. See note 66, below.

INDIANA HISTORICAL SOCIETY

[31] Stedman Whitwell, an English architect and social reformer, apparently a "man of parts" since he was involved in a variety of activities. He came to America with Robert Owen's party in the fall of 1825, and with Donald Macdonald (see below, note 95) edited the ship's paper "The Sextant." He wrote an ode called "Land of the West" which appeared in the last number with music furnished by Signor Manuel García (see below, note 86). In New York it was published under the title *Ebor Nova*, and in March 1826, was sung at a social meeting in New Harmony by several pupils of Mme Fretageot (see note 105, below).

On the second journey to America, in 1825-26, Whitwell and Macdonald had charge of a scale model of Robert Owen's proposed buildings formed as a phalanstery to be erected at New Harmony which they presented to President John Quincy Adams on December 3, 1825. Whitwell also devised a system of nomenclature, a proposal to develop place names by utilizing in a compound word the longitude and latitude of each locality. Letters were to be used instead of the usual numerals, and the first part of the name indicated latitude, the second longitude. The entire complicated system was described in *The New-Harmony Gazette*, April 12, 1826. *The Diaries of Donald Macdonald, 1824-1826* (Indiana Historical Society *Publications*, XIV, No. 2, Indianapolis, 1942), pp. 307, 320; Robert Dale Owen, *Threading My Way*, p. 263; Paul Brewster, "Three Songs from New Harmony," *Indiana Magazine of History*, XLVII (1951), 261-64; Hugh Hazelrigg, "Garcia and 'Land of the West,'" *Indiana Magazine of History*, XLVII (1951), 365-66; George B. Lockwood, *The New Harmony Movement* (New York, D. Appleton and Company, 1905), pp. 101-2, 114-15, 131; Wilson, *The Angel and the Serpent* (Indiana University Press, 1964), pp. 114-15, 154.

[32] The entry for this day down through the words "scarcely any beggars" is the basis for the part of the series by Robert Dale Owen entitled "The Dutch and Their Country," which appeared in *The New-Harmony Gazette*, November 22, 1826.

[33] In the article entitled "Destiny," in *The Free Enquirer*, January 15, 1831, cited above, note 2, Robert Dale Owen wrote: "His [Higgins'] sister was married to a worthy citizen, and a young and beautiful family promised them as much happiness as falls to the lot of mortals but mercantile reverses brought care and difficulty into their household, and the chill of poverty threatened to blight their future prospects." Robert Dale refers to Higgins' brother-in-law and sister as Mr. and Mrs. Fraser, below, p. 210.

[34] The organ was constructed between 1735 and 1738 by Christ Müller, with 3 keyboards, 60 stops, and 5,000 pipes.

[35] Robert Dale probably means Trippenhuis, a huge building erected in 1662 by the architect Justus Vingboons (Vinckeboons). The Royal Museum or Dutch Museum was transferred here in 1814 and then to the Ryks Museum which opened in 1885.

To Holland and To New Harmony

[36] A native of Leyden, Gerard Dou (1613-75) studied with Rembrandt and became best known for his genre paintings.

[37] A Dutch painter, Paul Potter (1625-54) was particularly famous for his depiction of animals. His best works are in the museums of Amsterdam and The Hague.

[38] Baron Menno van Coehoorn (or Coehorn) (1641-1704), Dutch soldier and military engineer, an expert on fortifications.

[39] The portion of this paragraph from this point through "excellent class of people" was incorporated in Robert Dale's article on "The Dutch and Their Country," in *The New-Harmony Gazette,* November 22, 1826.

[40] In the article entitled "Destiny," in *The Free Enquirer,* January 15, 1831, pp. 89-91, cited above, notes 2 and 33, which details the story of Carl Higgins, Robert Dale states that Carl was the idol of the social circle in which he moved, a fact which he attributed partly to Carl's brave rescue of a young girl and her brother from drowning when they went through the ice while skating. Robert Dale wrote, "I visited with him the scene of his exploit and accompanied him to the house of her whose life he had saved. . . . He received more than a son's welcome from the father, and more than a brother's from the pretty, interesting daughter."

According to Robert Dale's later account, Carl continued to be somber and moody. During one of his depressed moments he recounted a series of family misfortunes and Robert Dale tried to talk him out of his despondency and took him along on his visits to observe the Dutch communal colonies. On their return to Amsterdam they found that Carl's father had been appointed consul general to ——— (left blank in the story) and Carl vice-consul. Even this did not raise the young man's spirits. On parting from Robert Dale he said, "No, we shall not meet again. You will live; you will prosper; it is your fate. It is not mine." Four months later Robert Dale received word that both the father and Carl had died of a dread disease contracted on their journey to the consular posts awaiting them.

[41] The entire entry for June 18 and the entry for June 19 through the paragraph beginning "The education of the children . . ." are used in the article "The Dutch and Their Country," *The New-Harmony Gazette,* November 29, 1826. Here Robert Dale changes Dutch money into dollars and cents for the American reading public whereas in this journal (while he was still thinking as an Englishman) he translated the Dutch sums into pounds, shillings, and pence.

[42] The first of several colonies established in Holland in aid of the indigent poor. The economic depression that followed in the wake of the Napoleonic wars was felt keenly in the Netherlands, and as a means of alleviating the greatly increased pauperism a voluntary organization, the Benevolent Society of Holland, was set up in 1818 at the The Hague, which raised, through voluntary contributions, funds for the purchase of a 1,300-acre tract of uncultivated heath land to be known as "Fredericks-Oord" after the King's second son. Here was established an agricultural colony

INDIANA HISTORICAL SOCIETY

for unemployed workers and their families. Within the next few years a number of other colonies were established, all operated generally on the same plan.

It is of some interest to compare Robert Dale's 1825 description with those to be found in accounts by others published a few years later. See "Home Colonies," *The Quarterly Review* (London), XLI (1829), 522-50, and the more extensive *An Account of the Poor-Colonies and Agricultural Workhouses of the Benevolent Society of Holland. By a member of the Highland Society of Scotland* (Edinburgh, 1828).

[43] Superintendent of Philipp Emanuel von Fellenberg's school conducted for children of the poor classes at Hofwyl.

[44] A figure "2" is written above the 4 1/2.

[45] The article in *The New-Harmony Gazette* (November 29, 1826) reads ". . . each member of the society paying about *a dollar a year*. In pursuance of their object the society negotiates loans at (four?) per cent to a considerable amount. . . ."

[46] General Jan Van den Bosch (1780-1844). This officer had seen service in the East Indies and spent much time on the island of Java where he purchased an estate and entered with zeal into plans of agriculture. He was the author of a work published in Dutch entitled "On the Practicability of Instituting, in the Most Advantageous Manner, a General Pauper Establishment in the Kingdom of the Netherlands." *Quarterly Review* (London) XLI (1829), 540-41. He later (1830) became governor general of Batavia.

[47] The portion of the journal from this point through the words "*without assistance*" in the third paragraph below formed the basis for *The New-Harmony Gazette* article for December 6, 1826.

[48] Not found. The portion of the page of the journal where the plan was attached is now blank.

[49] The entry for June 20 was adapted for use in *The New-Harmony Gazette* for January 17, 1827. Most of the sums of money have been translated into dollars and cents in the *Gazette*.

[50] In *The New-Harmony Gazette* this reads "built of brick." In the journal "built" appears to be repeated.

[51] In *The New-Harmony Gazette* this reads ". . . a dollar, or a dollar and a quarter, an acre."

[52] In the *Gazette* article of January 17, 1827, Robert Dale converts the figures given here to dollars, the total expense for each family for buying the land, building the cottage, preparing the land, and purchasing the stock, furniture, etc., being $480, the weekly expense for each family being $2.00.

[53] This entry through the paragraph beginning "In the workhouse" was used for *The New-Harmony Gazette* article of January 24, 1827.

[54] This sentence, perhaps for the sake of delicacy, was omitted from the *Gazette* article.

To Holland and To New Harmony

[55] In the *Gazette* Robert Dale substituted "countries" for "England." This spirit of religious toleration is again noted by Robert Dale in the November 12, 1831, issue of *The Free Enquirer*, p. 24.

[56] "Drinking" is replaced by "intemperance in the use of ardent spirits" in the January 24, 1827, article in the *Gazette*.

[57] The Mauritshuis, erected between 1633 and 1644, since 1820 has served as one of the most famous of European museums.

[58] Perhaps Robert Dale meant to write Van Aelst. The work of still-life painter Willem van Aelst is represented in the museum in The Hague; however, the most famous flower paintings there are by Jan David de Heem.

[59] Cornelius Cels (1778-1859), painter of portraits and historical subjects.

[60] Peter Paul Rubens (1577-1640), renowned Flemish painter of, especially, historical and sacred subjects.

[61] This paragraph forms the introduction to the series "The Dutch and Their Country," in *The New-Harmony Gazette*, November 15, 1826.

[62] Booksellers and publishers located in the Strand.

[63] Probably Sir Isaac Lyon Goldsmid (1778-1859), financier and philanthropist and England's first Jewish baronet. He was a student of Owen's system of education at New Lanark where he spent some time when a young man as a guest of Owen, and he and his wife "trained and educated a family of eight, as nearly according to the system of New Lanark, as a conscientious adherence to the Jewish religion would admit." *The Life of Robert Owen by Himself*, pp. 207-8.

[64] Sir John Bowring (1792-1872), linguist, writer, traveler, member of Parliament, and literary executor of Jeremy Bentham (1748-1832), the British social philosopher and expounder of utilitarianism. Bowring served as an editor of and contributor to the *Westminster Review* founded by Bentham. *Dictionary of National Biography*, II, 984-88.

[65] Chester Harding (1792-1866), a self-taught American painter of portraits who, according to Leopold, executed a portrait of Robert Owen. Leopold states that Harding was present on the occasion of Richard Flower's visit to Owen when he described the Harmonist settlement in Indiana. Harding advised Owen to try out his experiment in an eastern state rather than in the West. *Robert Dale Owen*, pp. 17, 20.

[66] John Walker, a wealthy member of the Society of Friends and one of Owen's partners in the purchase of the New Lanark mills in 1813. See note 22, above, and *The Life of Robert Owen by Himself*, pp. 247-51. His brother Charles was manager of the mills after Robert Owen and Robert Dale Owen left. See correspondence in Owen Family Papers in the possession of Kenneth Dale Owen, particularly Anne Caroline Owen and Jane Owen, Holland Place, Glasgow, to their brothers [New Harmony], February 26, 1827; David Dale Owen, Holland Place, Glasgow, to his brothers, New Harmony, April 20, 1827; and Mrs. Robert Owen's renunciation of her claim to her husband's property in the United States, Glasgow, October 30, 1828. This last document states ". . . Before these witnesses Charles

Walker, one of the partners and at present manager of the Cotton Mills at New Lanark. . . . ." It is signed twice by Charles Walker. The Owen Family Papers are not available to researchers.

[67] At this time John Abel Smith (1802-1871), son of John Smith (note 6, above), was in Christ College, Cambridge, where he received an M.A. degree in 1827. He became the chief partner of the London banking firm of Smith, Payne, and Smith. Politically a liberal, he was a member of Parliament for many years. *Dictionary of National Biography,* XVIII, 490.

[68] The country house of John Walker at Southgate, Middlesex.

[69] The apollonicon, a unique organ of immense size having five keyboards and 1,900 pipes, invented in England in 1817 and a great attraction for twenty-five years.

[70] A citizen of Edinburgh and apparently a business associate of Robert Owen. In the Branigin–Owen Collection in the Library of the New Harmony Workingmen's Institute there are several letters to and from John Archibald Campbell (1788-1866) regarding money to be paid to Robert Owen from the David Dale estate. Boase, *Modern English Biography.*

[71] Anne Caroline Dale (Mrs. Robert) Owen (1778?-1831), the daughter of David Dale, owner of the New Lanark mills which Robert Owen and his partners acquired in 1799. She did not share her husband's intellectual and social interests and her life was based on a devout Presbyterianism as opposed to her husband's atheism. Due both to personal inclination and to increasingly poor health she did not join her husband in his American undertakings. She and her daughters remained at Braxfield until 1828, when Owen disposed of his New Lanark shares, and then moved into more modest quarters nearby. Letters in the Owen Family Papers in possession of Kenneth Dale Owen, refer to her recurring illness.

In a letter to her son William dated January 13 and 14, 1826, while Robert Dale was on his way to New Harmony, she wrote, "You may suppose us, now . . . as happy as circumstances will allow us, the distance of dear friends I find a great trial to me . . . and certainly the absence of my dear husband, and children, I feel very much, and notwithstanding you think the New System brings happiness, it certainly my dear William in the first instance, has created a great deal of uneasiness to *some individuals."* In her last years she seldom saw her husband. Her four sons all came to America—William in 1824, Robert Dale in 1825, Richard and David Dale in 1828. Robert Dale saw his mother only once more before her death, when he visited Scotland in 1827. Wilson, *The Angel and the Serpent,* p. 122; Podmore, *Robert Owen,* I, 48-55, II, 394; Margaret Cole, *Robert Owen of New Lanark* (New York, Oxford University Press, 1953), pp. 31-42, 160; G. D. H. Cole, *Robert Owen* (London, Ernest Benn, 1925), pp. 178-79.

[72] Robert Dale's sisters were Anne (1805?-1830), Jane (1806-1861), and Mary (?-1832). The oldest and the youngest and their mother all died within the period of a year and a half. Both Anne and Jane, after complet-

TO HOLLAND AND TO NEW HARMONY

ing their schooling in London, taught in the New Lanark schools and Jane, who came to America, in 1833, played a major role in the educational and social life of New Harmony during the remainder of her lifetime. She married Robert Fauntleroy there in 1835. Leopold, *Robert Dale Owen,* pp. 6, 112-13, 129; Owen Family Papers, in possession of Kenneth Dale Owen; Local History file, New Harmony Library of the Workingmen's Institute; Robert Dale Owen, New Harmony, to Richard Owen, January 10, 1861, copy in Library of Workingmen's Institute from original in private collection of Owen Armstrong. Lecture XIII of Robert Owen's *Lectures on an Entire New State of Society* (London, J. Brooks [1830], pp. 193-203), is devoted entirely to a description of Anne, her philosophy of life and educational ideas, and also furnishes some details of the early lives of the Owen children. See also Podmore, *Robert Owen,* II, 393-94. A moving poem by Jane in the Old Fauntleroy Home Manuscript Collection, New Harmony, points up vividly the strong bond between the two older sisters. A reference to Mary's death may be found in *The Crisis* (Robert Owen editor), I, No. 4, October 28, 1832.

[73] Moravian brethren, members of the Christian denomination (Unitas Fratrum) that traces its history back through the evangelical movement in Bohemia and Moravia to the doctrine expounded by John Huss. The community at Zeist was founded in 1746. The name Hernhouters or Herrnhutters derives from the town Herrnhut (meaning Watch of the Lord) in Saxony, Germany, which was founded by Count Nicklaus Ludwig von Zinzendorf as a refuge for the persecuted brethren. Begun in 1727, this religious community was particularly concerned in caring for the poor. The principal trade of the town was linen. There was no community of goods, each workman receiving wages for work done. *Encyclopedia of Religion and Ethics,* edited by James Hastings (12 volumes plus index. New York, Charles Scribner's Sons, 1908-27), VIII, 837-41.

[74] J. A. Hamilton, the younger, of Dalzell, whose lands at Motherwell were but a few miles from New Lanark. He was an early admirer and supporter of Owen's views. *The Life of Robert Owen by Himself,* pp. 329-30. A project for founding a model community at Motherwell collapsed when Robert Owen transferred his activities to America. Hamilton then became an associate with Abram Combe at Orbiston and lost his fortune in the enterprise. Podmore, *Robert Owen, passim.*

[75] Perhaps the J. Wright mentioned by Podmore as an old friend of the Owen family and Robert Owen's solicitor. *Robert Owen,* II, 394.

[76] The progress of the Orbiston community was detailed in Abram Combe's publication *The Register for the First Society of Adherents to Divine Revelation at Orbiston.* It describes the place, views, and occupations of the colonists, and frequently includes letters containing passages of public interest, several of which concern the New Harmony enterprise. The volume in the Library of the Workingmen's Institute includes issues from November 10, 1825, to May 9, 1827.

INDIANA HISTORICAL SOCIETY

77 A mile southwest from Braxfield a path ascends along the bank of the Clyde, here bordered by cliffs, rocks, and high hanging woods to Cora Linn, the finest of a series of falls, eighty-six feet, which dashes into a magnificent amphitheater of rocks. On the verge of the cliff are the ruins of Cora Castle, so-called after a legendary princess whose horse, startled by the noise of the falls, leaped with its mistress into the stream. The path leads about three quarters of a mile farther on to Bonnington Linn, a fall of thirty feet.

78 See note 24, regarding Margaret.

79 Claude Lorrain (1600-1682), professional name of the French landscapest, Claude Gellée, who called himself after his native province of Lorraine.

80 Sir Joshua Reynolds (1723-1792), the foremost fashionable portrait painter of his day, admired particularly for his studies of women and children.

81 The castle is perched on the edge and against the face of a cliff overhanging the North Esk. The oldest part dates from the early fourteenth century. It is said the ruins are only impressive when seen from the side next to the river.

82 Founded in 1446 by Sir William St. Clair, 3d Earl of Orkney and later Earl of Caithness, the chapel was intended to be the first part of a great collegiate church which was never completed.

83 The home of the Scottish poet of the Spenserian School, William Drummond (1585-1649), a picturesque castellated mansion built against a peel tower on a cliff above the glen of the North Esk surrounded by woods and gardens.

84 Located about one and a quarter miles west of Lanark, Cartland Crags are precipitous cliffs two hundred to four hundred feet high flanking a chasm on the Mouse River.

85 Probably the Joseph Applegath mentioned below, p. 253. In her letter to William Owen, January 13, 1826, cited above, note 71, Mrs. Owen wrote, "I was very astonished to hear that Mr. Applegath intended to leave his wife and proceed to New Harmony in the Spring. I shall cease to be astonished at anything now." Owen Family Papers. Karl Bernhard, Duke of Saxe-Weimar, who visited New Harmony in April 1826, mentioned in his *Travels* that towards evening on the 18th "an Englishman, a friend of Mr. Owen, Mr. Applegarth [*sic*] arrived, who had presided over the school in New Lanark, and was to organize one here in all probability." *Travels through North America, during the Years 1825 and 1826* (2 volumes in 1 volume. Philadelphia, Carey, Lea & Carey, 1828), II, 117-19.

86 Manuel de Popolo Vicente García (1775-1832), Spanish tenor, composer, and teacher, the idol of audiences in Paris and London. During his visit to the United States, 1825-1826, he gave seventy-nine performances in New York, including eleven operas new to America. Among his most celebrated pupils were his daughters Pauline Viardot-García and Maria Malibran. His son, mentioned later, Manuel Rodriguez García (1805-1906),

To Holland and To New Harmony

was a famous singing teacher in Paris and London, Jenny Lind being one of his pupils. *Encyclopedia of the Opera,* compiled by David Ewen, pp. 169-70. Robert Dale Owen recalled this musical family in *Threading My Way,* pp. 260-63. See note 31, above.

[87] See note 31, above, for mention of "The Sextant."

[88] Dr. William Price, who, with his wife Hannah Fisher Price and three children, was to join the "Boatload of Knowledge" bound for New Harmony. He was the son of the superintendent of the Friends' Boarding School in Westown near Philadelphia and brother of Dr. Philip M. Price, a Philadelphia physician already at New Harmony. Arthur E. Bestor, *Education and Reform at New Harmony, The Correspondence of William Maclure and Marie Duclos Fretageot* (Indiana Historical Society *Publications,* XV, No. 3, Indianapolis, 1948), pp. 303, 330; Wilson, *The Angel and the Serpent,* p. 129.

[89] A picture of New Harmony in this period before Robert Owen's return may be found in Thomas C. Pears, Jr. (ed.), *New Harmony, An Adventure in Happiness: Papers of Thomas and Sarah Pears* (Indiana Historical Society *Publications,* XI, No. 1, Indianapolis, 1933). See also the letters of William Pelham written from New Harmony in Lindley (comp.), *Indiana as Seen by Early Travelers* (*Indiana Historical Collections* [III], Indianapolis, 1916), pp. 368-417. The Pelham letters have been deposited in the Library of the Workingmen's Institute Special Collections.

[90] A merchant and ship owner, Jeremiah Thompson (1784-1835) was at this time one of the proprietors of the Liverpool packet line which included the "Pacific," "Amity," "Courier," and "James Monroe." He perhaps overexpanded his business interests, for by 1828 he was insolvent. However, through his establishment of the first scheduled sailings of packets out of New York he is regarded as bringing preeminence to New York City as a seaport. He was a Quaker. *Dictionary of American Biography* (22 volumes. New York, Charles Scribner's Sons, 1928-37), XVIII, 461.

[91] As governor of New York (1817-1828) DeWitt Clinton (1769-1828) was, as Robert Dale says, largely responsible for the construction of the Erie Canal which was opened on November 4, just two days before the Owen party landed. Clinton had served in the New York legislature and as mayor of New York, and was defeated by James Madison in a bid for the Presidency in 1812. *Ibid.,* IV, 221-25; *Diaries of Donald Macdonald,* p. 308.

[92] The Quaker minister who was largely responsible for the separation in Quaker communities in 1827 and 1828 between the Orthodox and the more liberal Hicksites. Hicks (1748-1830) was strongly antislavery. *Dictionary of American Biography,* IX, 6-7.

[93] These were, in fact, three Sistare sisters, Lucy, Frances, and Sarah, pupils of Mme Fretageot, who were to join Robert Dale and others on board the "Philanthropist," bound for New Harmony. The Duke of Saxe-Weimar describes the sisters in his *Travels through North America,* II,

INDIANA HISTORICAL SOCIETY

117-19. Lucy (1801-1886) married the entomologist Thomas Say. See below, note 102, and Harry B. Weiss and Grace Ziegler, *Thomas Say: Early American Naturalist* (Springfield, Ill., Charles C. Thomas, 1931). Lucy signed the name as "Sistare." Josephine M. Elliott, "The Owen Family Papers," in *Indiana Magazine of History*, LX (1964), 336.

[94] Mrs. Fisher would be another passenger on the "Philanthropist." The Duke of Saxe-Weimar, in recounting his visit to New Harmony in April 1826, in his *Travels*, mentions her as "a Madam F——, a native of St. Petersburg. She married an American merchant, settled there, and had the misfortune to lose her husband three days after marriage. She then joined her husband's family at Philadelphia, and as she was somewhat eccentric and sentimental, quickly became enthusiastically attached to Mr. Owen's system. She told me, however, in German, that she found herself egregiously deceived; that the highly vaunted equality was not altogether to her taste; that some of the society were too low, and the table was below all criticism." *Travels through North America*, II, 112. Mrs. Fisher may have been a sister-in-law of Hannah Fisher Price, wife of Dr. William Price. See note 88, above, and Bestor, *Education and Reform at New Harmony*, p. 330n.

[95] Captain Donald Macdonald of the Royal Engineers (1791-1872) became interested in Robert Owen's theories and his work at New Lanark, was associated with the beginnings of the community that developed into Orbiston, and accompanied Robert Owen to Ireland in 1822. He journeyed to America with Robert Owen in 1824 and 1825 and accompanied him on this second trip to America. This is the first mention of Macdonald by Robert Dale, although he had been with the party from the start. Macdonald's *Diaries* are invaluable for their firsthand accounts. Biographical material on Macdonald is given in Caroline Dale Snedecker's introduction to the *Diaries*.

[96] John Griscom (1774-1852), teacher and scientist, had a very early interest in Pestalozzian theories and practices of education. He conducted a private school of science in New York City (1808-1818) and during 1818 and 1819 he traveled in Europe to study educational institutions, including Pestalozzi's establishment at Yverdon, Fellenberg's at Hofwyl, and Owen's at New Lanark, and visited the poor colonies of Holland. In 1825 he reorganized his New York City school into the New York High School for boys which featured particularly fine equipment for the study of science and a new stress on gymnastics. He was one of the founders of the New York Society for the Prevention of Pauperism and the Society for the Reformation of Juvenile Delinquents and aided in the establishment of the first American reformatory. Will S. Monroe, *History of the Pestalozzian Movement in the United States* (Syracuse, N.Y., C. W. Bardeen, 1907), pp. 207-8; *Dictionary of American Biography*, VIII, 7.

[97] Thomas Hulme (1777-1855), engineer and inventor. A native of England, he became an enterprising citizen of Philadelphia. He was in

To Holland and To New Harmony

large measure responsible for that city's Fairmount Water Works and was a leading figure in the construction of the Louisville and Portland Canal at the Falls of the Ohio. Thompson Westcott (comp.), *Biographies of Philadelphians* (1866), I, pt. 2, p. 336. According to Macdonald, Hulme had arrived from France the previous evening and was visiting his daughter in New York. *Diaries*, p. 309.

[98] Samuel Spackman, Owen's financial agent in Philadelphia and later the agent for the *New-Harmony Gazette*.

[99] Dr. James Rush (1786-1869), physician and scientist of Philadelphia, son of Dr. Benjamin Rush, physician and signer of the Declaration of Independence, and brother of Dr. Richard Rush, statesman and diplomat, who at this time was serving as Secretary of the Treasury.

[100] The Philadelphia Academy of Natural Sciences, founded in 1812. William Maclure (see note 101, below) served as its president from 1817 until his death in 1840.

[101] William Maclure (1763-1840), the principal associate and financial partner of Robert Owen in the development of New Harmony. His activities in the fields of education and science led him into social reform, culminating in the establishment of the School of Industry and the Workingmen's Institute. It was Maclure's reputation that attracted the scientists and educators who came to New Harmony on the "Philanthropist." Bestor, *Education and Reform at New Harmony, passim;* Samuel George Morton, *A Memoir of William Maclure, Esq.* (Philadelphia, 1844).

[102] Thomas Say (1789-1834) was librarian of the Academy of Natural Sciences when Robert Owen first met him. It was his long-time friendship for Maclure, however, which was responsible for his coming to New Harmony, where he remained until his death. His works on American entomology and conchology gained him a lasting reputation. The young Lucy Sistare (see above, note 93) became his wife on January 4, 1827. Weiss and Ziegler, *Thomas Say*.

[103] Reuben Haines (1786-1831), corresponding secretary of the Academy of Natural Sciences from 1813 until his death. He was interested in science generally but not a specialist in any branch. *Guide to the Manuscript Collections in the Academy of Natural Sciences of Philadelphia* (Academy of Natural Sciences of Philadelphia, *Special Publication No. 5*, 1963), p. 196.

[104] Perhaps Washington Smith, mentioned by Macdonald in his diary of the previous trip to America. *Diaries of Donald Macdonald*, p. 209.

[105] Marie Duclos Fretageot (1783-1833), a Pestalozzian teacher whom Maclure attracted to the school in Philadelphia originally started by Joseph Neef (see note 134, below). Mme Fretageot came to New Harmony and assumed charge of Maclure's educational enterprises and in time became his trusted business agent. The exchange of letters between Mme Fretageot and Maclure over a fifteen-year period comprises perhaps the most significant contemporary record available of the Owen experiment in communal life. A selection of these letters is in Bestor, *Education and Reform*

INDIANA HISTORICAL SOCIETY

at *New Harmony*. See also Local History file in the Library of the New Harmony Workingmen's Institute, for biographical material on Mme Fretageot.

[106] Charles Alexandre Lesueur (1778-1846), naturalist and scientist, artist and teacher. As a young man he joined the Napoleonic scientific expedition to Australia and discovered many zoological species. In 1816 he came to America with Maclure and served as curator for the Academy of Natural Sciences for seven years. After coming to New Harmony he taught art and natural science in the community schools. Considered by his peers a great ichthyologist, he is probably better remembered for his many sketches and water colors of the American scene. Over twelve hundred are to be found at the Muséum d'Histoire Naturelle, Le Havre, France, where Lesueur returned to become director in 1837, after the deaths of his dear friends Say and Maclure. Adrien Loir, *Charles-Alexandre Lesueur* . . . (Le Havre, Muséum d'Histoire Naturelle, 1920); E. T. Hamy, *Les Voyages du Naturaliste Ch. Alex. Lesueur dans l'Amérique du Nord (1815-1837)* (Journal de la Société des Américanistes de Paris, V, 1904); R. W. G. Vail, *The American Sketchbooks of Charles Alexandre Lesueur 1816-1837* (Worcester, Mass., American Antiquarian Society, 1938).

[107] A private library organized in 1814, located at this time in Philosophical Hall.

[108] In 1786 Charles Willson Peale (1741-1827), portrait painter, scientist, and inventor, opened the Peale Museum in Independence Hall devoted to fine arts and natural history. Of his seventeen children, Raphael, Rembrandt, Rubens, Franklin, and Titian Ramsay became painters. Franklin, Titian Ramsay, and Rubens co-operated in the management of the museum.

[109] Macdonald mentions meeting at Dr. Rush's "a Miss Roach an English lady who lives with her brother at Bedford, Massachusetts. He is a great advocate for the new system." *Diaries of Donald Macdonald*, p. 313.

[110] Described by Macdonald as "a Scotch schoolmaster." *Ibid.*, 314

[111] Described by Donald Macdonald as the wife of a former commander of a Liverpool packet and extremely interested in Robert Owen's ideas. *Ibid.*

[112] Joseph Bonaparte (or Buonaparte) (1768-1844), brother of Napoleon I and king of Naples, 1806-1808, and of Spain, 1803-1813, resided in the United States from 1815 to 1832. His nephew, Charles Lucien Bonaparte, was a naturalist, author of *American Ornithology, or History of Birds Inhabiting the United States Not Given by Wilson* (1825-33). For another account of this visit see *Diaries of Donald Macdonald*, pp. 315-16. The Bonaparte residence was on the Delaware River a half mile from Bordentown.

[113] Nothing has been found about Sarah Turner although she is listed by both Macdonald and Lesueur as a passenger. See Wilson, *The Angel and the Serpent*, p. 140, for a comment on varying recordings and transcriptions of her name.

To Holland and To New Harmony

[114] Guillaume Sylvan Casimir Phiquepal d'Arusmont (1779-1855), a teacher trained in the Pestalozzian system and sponsored by Maclure along with Mme Fretageot and Joseph Neef. In the United States he was known as William S. Phiquepal. He taught in the New Harmony schools and returned to Paris in 1831 where he married Frances Wright, the reformer and feminist. Bestor, *Education and Reform at New Harmony, passim;* Local History file in the New Harmony Library of the Workingmen's Institute. Victor Duclos lists five passengers as Phiquepal's pupils including himself. See below, pp. 266-67. His list, however, includes at least ten children.

[115] The man servant of the Owens, called Smith by Lesueur and Macdonald. The Duke of Saxe-Weimar, recounting his visit to New Harmony in his *Travels,* says of him, ". . . I received a visit from one of the German patriots who had entered the society, of the name of Schmidt, who wished to have been considered as first lieutenant in the Prussian artillery, at Erfurt. He appeared to have engaged in one of the political conspiracies there, and to have deserted. Mr. Owen brought him from England last autumn as a servant. He was now a member of the society, and had charge of the cattle. His fine visions of freedom seemed to be very much lowered, for he presented himself to me, and his father to Mr. Huygens, to be employed as servants." *Travels in North America,* II, 119.

[116] A Swiss artist, a member of the party accompanying Mme Fretageot from Paris to Philadelphia in 1823. He was the butt of many a schoolboy prank in New Harmony. "Diary and Recollections of Victor Colin Duclos," in Lindley (comp.), *Indiana as Seen by Early Travelers,* pp. 536-46. The original manuscript of Duclos' Diary and Recollections is in the Library of the New Harmony Workingmen's Institute Special Collections. Wilson says the artist's last name was spelled variously, but probably was Abeonesser. Wilson, *The Angel and the Serpent,* p. 139.

[117] Victor Dupalais, a brother of Virginia Dupalais who was left sick at Pittsburgh but would board the "Philanthropist" on January 7. See below, p. 256, and *Diaries of Donald Macdonald,* pp. 333, 334. They had come to Philadelphia from Paris in the party with Mme Fretageot. "Diary and Recollections of Victor Colin Duclos," in Lindley (comp.), *Indiana as Seen by Early Travelers,* p. 536.

[118] For a comparison of Robert Dale's passenger list with those of others see below, pp. 265-68.

[119] The community established by the Rappites on their return to Pennsylvania after the sale of their community of Harmonie, Indiana, to Robert Owen. Their first community in America was at Harmonie, Pennsylvania.

[120] George Rapp (1757-1847), founder of the Harmony Society (Harmonists or Rappites), a German pietistic sect. The first group of Harmonists arrived in America from Würtemberg in 1804. Karl J. R. Arndt,

George Rapp's Harmony Society, 1785-1847 (Philadelphia, University of Pennsylvania Press, 1965).

[121] Frederick Rapp (1775-1834), adopted son of George Rapp and the business agent for the Harmony Society. The great economic success of the Society was due in large measure to his fine business acumen. He served in the Indiana Constitutional Convention in 1816 and was a member of the board of commissioners appointed to locate the site of the seat of government of the State of Indiana. Arndt, *George Rapp's Harmony Society, passim*.

[122] Granddaughter of George Rapp, Gertrude Rapp (1809-1889) was described by Donald Macdonald when he met her at Harmonie, Indiana, in his 1824-1825 journey to America, as "pretty, mild, amiable, and pleasing. She sang a few little German songs in an unaffected manner, & was a fine specimen in her own manners, how charming, simple, innocent & interesting a character a Harmonie life is capable of producing." *Diaries of Donald Macdonald*, p. 259. She was also described by William Owen (see note 123, below). *Diary of William Owen from November 10, 1824, to April 20, 1825* (Indiana Historical Society *Publications*, IV, No. 1, Indianapolis, 1906), pp. 75, 77, 89.

[123] This is Robert Dale's first mention of his younger brother, William (1802-42), who had accompanied his father to America in 1824 and remained at Harmonie (New Harmony) when the latter returned to England. *Diary of William Owen*. After the collapse of the community he continued to live in New Harmony.

[124] François Marie Charles Fourier (1772-1837), French socialist and proponent of a social reform system (Fourierism) which proposed the division of the world's population into small co-operative groups for economic production and maintenance, the achievement of social justice, and fulfillment of individual desires.

[125] Perhaps Caleb Lowns (Lownes) who was associated with the community founded at Yellow Springs, Ohio. Arthur E. Bestor, *Backwoods Utopias. The Sectarian and Owenite Phases of Communitarian Socialism in America: 1663-1829* (Philadelphia, University of Pennsylvania Press, 1950), p. 213. It is possible this is the Caleb Lownes who was in Vincennes around 1815 to 1818 and who died in 1828 aged seventy-four. "From Old Vincennes, 1815," edited by Chase C. Mooney, in *Indiana Magazine of History*, LVII (1961), 141-54. (Professor Mooney transcribed the name mistakenly as Townes.) This Lownes had been active in prison reform in Philadelphia. Negley K. Teeters, "Caleb Lownes of Philadelphia: 1754-1828," in *The Prison Journal* (Philadelphia), XLIII (1963), 10-11.

[126] Mrs. Fisher apparently joined Robert Owen and accompanied him to Yellow Springs, Ohio, and on to New Harmony. Donald Macdonald recorded that on reaching Cincinnati January 17, the party on board the "Philanthropist" found "that Mr. Owen had left that place [Cincinnati] 10 days before in a steamboat with Mrs. Fisher. He had been 60 miles up the

TO HOLLAND AND TO NEW HARMONY

country at the Yellow Springs community on the forks of the Miami river, which had partly suspended its operations in consequences of a want of funds." *Diaries of Donald Macdonald*, p. 335. For an account of the Yellow Springs community see Bestor, *Backwoods Utopias*, pp. 210-13.

[127] A description of the community costume finally adopted is given by the Duke of Saxe-Weimar in his *Travels in North America*, II, 111; see also Pears (ed.), *New Harmony, An Adventure in Happiness*, p. 82. A picture of Frances Wright in the costume is in A. J. G. Perkins and Theresa Wolfson, *Frances Wright, Free Enquirer* . . . (New York, Harper & Brothers, 1939), facing p. 88.

[128] See note 117, above.

[129] See note 31, above, relative to Whitwell, Macdonald, and the model.

[130] Benjamin Tappan (1773-1857), antislavery leader, judge of the 5th Ohio circuit (1816-1823), and United States senator (1839-45). The son mentioned here was Benjamin. *Dictionary of American Biography*, XVIII, 300-301.

[131] Probably Victor Duclos. However, in his "Diary and Recollections" he does not mention this incident. He does recall that while the boat was stuck in the ice "two of the French students broke through the ice while skating and came near drowning." Lindley (comp.), *Indiana as Seen by Early Travelers*, p. 538. See above, pp. 242-43.

[132] This may be the William McArthur whose name appears in the New Harmony Community Petty Journal 1, June 27, 1825—July 27, 1826, p. 237, where are listed under date of January 28, 1826, the charges at the tavern for the passengers from the "Philanthropist." See below, pp. 267-68. The Journal is in the Library of the New Harmony Workingmen's Institute.

[133] John Cleves Symmes (d. 1829), nephew of the founder of Cincinnati and proponent of the theory of concentric spheres. He claimed that the earth was hollow inside with the likelihood of its being habitable. An opening located in North America near the North Pole allowed the moon to force air in and out. Symmes explained that the hot air expelled accounted for the dark complexion of the Eskimo. He sought aid from various learned societies in support of a polar expedition to prove his theory. R. Carlyle Buley, *The Old Northwest, 1815-1840* (2 volumes. Indiana Historical Society, Indianapolis, 1950), II, 594.

[134] Francis Joseph Nicholas Neef (1770-1854), a Pestalozzian teacher, came to Philadelphia in 1806 and, under the patronage of William Maclure, founded the first Pestalozzian school in the United States. In 1814 Neef had a school near Louisville, but by this time had abandoned teaching and was farming. On January 27, 1826, Maclure wrote to Neef from New Harmony: "I arrived here two days ago. . . . I could wish you to be here and have been contriving howe you could be enabled to come immidiately without your pecuniary interest suffiring. . . . Madam Fretageot is an excellent manager of the Girls and infants school but Phiquepal is a little too theoretical for the practical and usefull instruction that alone can

INDIANA HISTORICAL SOCIETY

benifit this society. . . . ." Copy in Library of the New Harmony Workingmen's Institute, of original letter in the private collection of Owen Armstrong. Bestor, *Education and Reform at New Harmony, passim.*

APPENDIX

[1] See above, pp. 178, 237. In his autobiography *Threading My Way*, pp. 267-68, Robert Dale Owen recalled only a few of his fellow passengers: "In the course of two or three weeks several pleasant and intelligent people had joined us . . . among them Thomas Say." He also remembered Charles Lesueur, Gerard Troost, and Miss Sistare and her two sisters. "Whether William Maclure . . accompanied us, or came on a few weeks later, I am not quite certain."

[2] *Diaries of Donald Macdonald*, p. 334. It should be remembered that Macdonald did not board the "Philanthropist" until January 7. He was accompanied by Whitman Stedwell. Macdonald states that Robert Owen and Mrs. Fisher had left the boat to proceed overland.

[3] "Diary and Recollections," in Lindley (comp.), *Indiana as Seen by Early Travelers*, p. 537.

[4] E. T. Hamy, *Les Voyages du Naturaliste Ch. Alex. Lesueur dans L'Amérique du Nord*, pp. 50-51. Hamy gives as his source a manuscript volume of Lesueur in the Muséum d'Histoire Naturelle, Le Havre: Esquisses et croquis des lieux où nous avons passé depuis le départ de Philadelphie à Pittsburg et de Pittsburg à New-Harmony pendant notre navigation à bord du *quille boat* en descendant l'Ohio depuis le 27 novembre 1825 jusqu'au 26 janvier 1826.

INDEX

INDEX

(* indicates identification note)

Abeonesser, Balthazar, 237, 265, 267, 268, *285.
Adams, John Quincy, 257, 274.
Allen, William, 184, 270, 272, *273.
Amersfoort (Holland), 193.
Amsterdam (Holland), 188-90, 209.
Apeldoorn (Holland), 193.
Applegath, Miss ——, 183.
Applegath, Joseph, 223, 224, 253, *280.
Arno's Grove, country home of John Walker, 215, *278.

Baarn (Holland), 191-92.
Barclay, ——, of New York, 228.
Barclay, George, of the New York firm of Barclay and Livingston, 230, 234.
Barnes, Thomas, 185, *273.
Barry, ——, teacher in New Lanark school, 220.
Beal, John, and family, 266, 267, 268.
Beaver (Pa.), 242, 251, 252, 257.
Bedford (Pa.), 237.
Bennebroek (Holland), 187, 209, 210.
Bennett, Capt. ——, of the SS "New York," 234.
Bentham, Jeremy, 214, 272, 277.
Blind, institution for, in Amsterdam, 188-89.
Bonaparte (Buonaparte), Charles Lucien, 234-35, *284.
Bonaparte (Buonaparte), Mrs. Charles Lucien, 235.

Bonaparte (Buonaparte), Joseph, 234, 235, *284.
Bonnington Linn, 220, 280.
Bowring, John, 214, *277.
Braxfield, Owen home near New Lanark, 175, 176, 181, 216, 278.
Bromley, seat of Joseph Foster, 215, 272.
Brougham, Henry Peter, Baron Brougham and Vaux, 182, 270, *271.

Camac, ——, of Philadelphia, 228.
Camac, [Turner?], of Philadelphia, 232, 233.
Campbell, Mrs. ——, 216.
Campbell, John Archibald, 216, *278.
Campbell, William, 181.
Carlisle (England), 224.
Castle Garden, New York City, 229-30.
Cels, Cornelius, 211, *277.
Chambersburg (Pa.), 237.
Chapeaurouge, Philipp, 182, 213.
Chartres, ——, 228.
Chase, ——, 266.
Chase, Mrs. ——, 266.
Christian Evidence Society, 183.
Cincinnati (Ohio), 262.
Clark, ——, of Cincinnati, 262.
Clibborn, Joshua, New York merchant, 234.
Clinton, DeWitt, 229, *281.
Coehorn (Coehoorn), Menno van, Baron, 191, *275.

291

Combe, Abram, 181, 216, *269-70, 279.
Combe, Andrew, 269.
Combe, George, 269.
Cora Castle, 220, 280.
Cowper, Miss ———, 183.
Cowper, Edward, 183, 184, *271.

Dale, David, 278.
Dalkeith House, 221.
Dana family, of near Marietta, 260.
Dou, Gerard, 190, *275.
Downing, ———, 228.
Drummond, William, 280.
Duclos, Peter L., 267.
Duclos, Victor C., 267.
Dufour, Amedie, 267.
Dupalais, Victor, 237, 256, 259, 265, 266, 267, *285, 287.
Dupalais, Virginia, 256, 265, 266, 268, *285.
Dutch, characterized by Robert Dale Owen, 186, 188, 212.

Economy (Pa.), 239-40, 256, 257.
Edinburgh (Scotland), 181, 216, 222.
Erie Canal, 229, 281.

Falque, Charles, 267.
Fauntleroy, Robert, 279.
Fellenberg, Philipp Emanuel von, 175, 271, 276.
Fisher, Mrs. [Helen?], 230, 231, 237, 245, 265, *282, 286-87, 288.
Fisler, Mme ———, 188, 190.
Fisler, M. W., 209.
Flower, Richard, 277.
Ford, ———, 209.
Foster, Joseph, 184, 215, *272.
Fourier, François Marie Charles, 240-49 *passim*, 255, *286.
Fox, Joseph, 272.
Fraser, ———, sister of Higgins, 187, 210.
Fraser, ———, of Bennebroek, 210.
Fraser, ———, of Baarn, 191, 192.

Fraser, Henri, of Amsterdam, 188, 209.
Fredericks-Oord, Dutch pauper colony, 194-200, 275-76.
Free Enquirer, 269, 274.
Freischütz, Der, 182, *271.
Fretageot, A. E., 266.
Fretageot, Marie Duclos, 240, 251-56 *passim*, 259, *283-84, 285, 287; passenger on "Philanthropist," 237, 265-68; Robert Dale Owen's opinion of, 177-78, 232, 246-47.

García, Manuel de Popolo Vicente, 224, 228, 274, *280-81.
García, Manuel Rodriguez, 228, 280.
Gibbs, Michael, 184, 213, *272.
Glasgow (Scotland), 219.
Glimmer, Mme ———, 192.
Goldschmid, Sir Isaac Lyon, 213, *277.
Gray, John, of Galashiels, 184, *273.
Greensburg (Pa.), 237.
Griscom, John, 230, *282.

Haarlem, 187-88, 209.
Hague, The, 210-11.
Haines, Reuben, 231, *283.
Hale, Miss ———, 267.
Hamilton, ———, 228.
Hamilton, Miss ———, 184.
Hamilton, J. A., of Dalzell, 219, 220, *279.
Hanbury, Cornelius, 184, *273.
Harding, Chester, 214, 215, *277.
Harloff, ———, 206-208.
Harmonie (Ind.), *see* New Harmony.
Harmonie (Pa.), 285.
Harmonists (Rappites), 175, 285; at Economy, 239-40.
Harrisburg (Pa.), 235.
Hart, ———, of London, 181, 183, 215.
Harvey, Jacob, New York merchant, 229.

INDEX

Hawthornden, home of William Drummond, 222, *280.
Hayward, ——, of Charleston, 228.
Hernhouters (Hernnhutters), colony at Zeist, 217, *279.
Herring, William, 268.
Hicks, Elias, 229, *281.
Higgins, [Carl?], 181, 182, 185, 186, 187, 188, 191, 192, 208, 209, *269, 275.
Hofwyl (Switzerland), 175, 195, 247, 271.
Holland, pauper colonies, 194-208, 275-76; Robert Dale Owen visits, 176, 185-212.
Hulme, Thomas, 230, 231, 232, 234, *282-83.
Hunt, Mr. and Mrs. ——, of Liverpool, 225.
Hunt, Leigh, 184, 225, *272.

Infant schools, 181-82, 270.
Irving, Edward, 181, *271.

Jones, ——, of India House, 214.

Kemmis, Mrs. ——, 183, 215.
Keverberg, Charles Louis Guillaume Joseph, Baron de, 218.

Lambton, Charles William, 184, 272.
Lawrence, Sir Thomas, 184, *272.
Lawrie, ——, 228.
Lepard, John, 183, 213, 215, *271.
Lesueur, Charles Alexandre, 232, 237, 239, 243, 244, 256, 265-68, *284, 288.
Lewis, Mr. and Mrs. ——, 232.
Liverpool (England), 224-26.
London (England), 181-85, 213-15.
London Co-operative Society, 183, 184, *272.
London Infant School Society, *270.
Lorrain, Claude, 221, *280.
Louisville (Ky.), 263.
Lowns (Lownes), Caleb, 245, *286.
Lynch, ——, of New York, 228.

McArthur, William, 268, *287.
McCarter, William, 259.
Macdonald, Donald, 256-57, 274, *282, 288; passenger on "Philanthropist," 257, 265-68; Robert Dale Owen's reaction to, 178, 257-58, 262.
Macfarlane, ——, 234, *284.
Maclure, William, 231, 232, 233, 239, 251-56 *passim*, 259, *283, 285, 287; passenger on "Philanthropist," 237, 265-68, 269; Robert Dale Owen's reaction to, 178, 247, 249.
Malibran, Maria, 280.
Margaret (Jessie), object of Robert Dale Owen's early romance, 176, 178, 184, *272-73.
Marietta (Ohio), 259, 260.
Maysville (Ky.), 260.
Meppel (Holland), 194.
Moffat, Mrs. ——, 216.
Morgan, John Minter, 181, 183, 213, 214, *270.
Morrison, James, 181, 213, *270.
Motherwell (Scotland), 279.
Mt. Vernon (Ind.), 264.
Muiden (Muyden), 190-91.
Mülder, ——, 195, 196.

Naarden (Holland), 191, 209.
Neef, Francis Joseph Nicholas, 263, 285, *287-88.
New Harmony (Harmonie, Ind.), 229, 264, 281; purchased by Robert Owen, 175; community costume, 246, 287; model for proposed buildings, 257, 274; School of Industry, 283; Workingmen's Institute, 283.
New-Harmony Gazette, articles on poor colonies of Holland, 177, 269, 274, 275, 276-77.
New Lanark (Scotland), 175, 176, 270, 277, 278; Owen's partners in acquisition of mills at, 1813, 272, 273, 277; schools, 223, 270, 279.

293

New Orleans (La.), 233, 234.
New South Wales, 214.
New York (N. Y.), 220-30, 233-34.
Norton, ——, 220.

Ommerschans (Omerschanz), colony for beggars in Holland, 203, 206-208.
Orbiston, co-operative community near Glasgow, 219-20, 270, 279.
Owen, Anne, sister of Robert Dale Owen, 176, 216, *278-79.
Owen, Anne Caroline Dale (Mrs. Robert), 175, 176, 216, 222, 253, *278.
Owen, David Dale, brother of Robert Dale Owen, 278.
Owen, Jane, sister of Robert Dale Owen, 176, 216, *278-79.
Owen, Mary, sister of Robert Dale Owen, 176, 216, *278-79.
Owen, Richard, brother of Robert Dale Owen, 278.
Owen, Robert, 176, 225, 239, 245, 262; purchases New Harmony, 175; criticized by Robert Dale Owen, 178, 228, 233-34; visits Elias Hicks, 229; visits Wilmington, 232; conducts meetings in Philadelphia, 235; passenger on "Philanthropist," 237, 265, 267; leaves "Philanthropist," 240, 288; partners of, in acquisition of New Lanark mills, 1813, 272; *American Discourses,* 273; portrait by Chester Harding, 277; visits Yellow Springs, 286-87.
Owen, Robert Dale, birth and education, 175; declares intention of becoming American citizen, 176; records passengers on "Philanthropist," 177, 178, 265-66, 288; later career and death, 179; in London, 181-85, 213-15; in Holland, 185-212; describes diorama,

213-14; journey to America, 224-29; in New York, 229-30, 233-34; journey from New York to Philadelphia, 231; in Philadelphia, 231-33, 235; journey from Philadelphia to Pittsburgh, 236-37; passenger on "Philanthropist," 237, 266, 267, 268; journey from Pittsburgh to Mt. Vernon, 237-64; reads Fourier, 240-49 *passim,* 255; at Safe Harbor, 242-59; goes hunting, 242, 244, 247, 248, 249, 252, 255; on proper care of rifle, 249-50, 254; attends shooting match, 250-51; arrives at Mt. Vernon and New Harmony, 264.
Owen, William, brother of Robert Dale Owen, 175, 176, 240, 278, *286.

Paupers, colonies for, in Holland, 194-208, 275-76.
Peale, Charles Willson, 232, *284.
Penn, ——, or Baarn, 192, 209.
Penrose, Mark, 266.
Pestalozzi, Johann Heinrich, educational theories, 175, 271, 282, 283, 285, 286.
Philadelphia (Pa.), 231-33, 235.
Philadelphia Academy of Natural Sciences, 231, *283.
"Philanthropist," keelboat, 176; passengers on board, 177, 237, 265-68, 269, 288; description of, 237; crew, 237, 247-48, 249; goes aground on Merriman's riffle, 239; detained by ice at Safe Harbor, 241-59.
Phillips, Thomas, 183, *272.
Phiquepal d'Arusmont, Guillaume Sylvan Casimir, 239, *285, 287; passenger on "Philanthropist," 237, 265-68; accident and subsequent illness, 243-48 *passim*, 251, 255-56.

INDEX

Pittsburgh (Pa.), 235-37.
Plough Court, London, seat of William Allen, 181, 184, 213, 215, *270.
Poor colonies, *see* Paupers, colonies for.
Post, Henry, officer of Franklin Bank, New York, 234.
Potter, Paul, 190, 211, *275.
Price, Hannah Fisher (Mrs. William), 237, 245, 265, 266, 267, 282.
Price, Philip M., 281.
Price, William, 229, 230, 231, 242, 244, 254-57 *passim*, *281; passenger on the "Philanthropist," 237, 265, 266, 267.
Prime, ——, of New York, 228.

Rapp, Frederick, 239, *286. ,
Rapp, George, 175, 239, *285-86.
Rapp, Gertrude, 239, *286.
Rappites, *see* Harmonists.
Rathbone, Richard, 224.
Rathbone, William, 224, 225.
Reynolds, Sir Joshua, 221, *280.
Rice, John, 244, 245, 249, 250, 254, 256.
Richmond, ——, 184.
Roche (Roach), Miss ——, 233, *284.
Rodgers, ——, 228.
Rosslyn Castle, 221, 222.
Rotterdam (Holland), 185-86, 211.
Rubens, Peter Paul, 211, *277.
Rush, Benjamin, 283.
Rush, James, 231, 233, *283.
Rush, Richard, 283.

Say, Thomas, 231, 233, 262, 282, *283; passenger on "Philanthropist," 237, 265-68, 288; Robert Dale Owen's reaction to, 247; on the American Indian, 251.
Schmidt (Smith), [Charles?], Owen's manservant, 237, 244, 245, 265-68, *285.

"Sextant, The," 227, 274.
Silvester, ——, of London, 183, 185, 213, 215.
Simpson, Mrs. ——, of Leith, 222.
Sistare (Sistaire, etc.), Frances, 230, 237, 248, 265, 266, *281, 288.
Sistare (Sistaire, etc.), Lucy, 230, 237, 265, 266, 268, *281-82, 283, 288.
Sistare (Sistaire), Sarah, 230, 237, 265, 266, *281, 288.
Skene, G. R., 270-71.
Skene, Philip Orkney, 181, 183, 184, 209, *270-71; account of visit to Zeist and Voorsel, 216-19.
Sketchley, Mrs. ——, 234, *284.
Slaughter, ——, of Leicester Square, London, 214.
Small, ——, of Edinburgh, 216.
Smith, [Charles?], *see* Schmidt.
Smith, John, 181, 183, 214, *270.
Smith, John Abel, 215, *278.
Smith, Washington, 232, *283.
Society for the Diffusion of Useful Knowledge, 271.
Somerset House, 184, *272.
Spackman, Samuel, 231, 255, *283.
Speakman, John, and family, 267.
Spencer, Ephraim, 255.
Steubenville (Ohio), 255, 256, 259.
Stewart, ——, of Louisville, 263.
Stewart, Mary Dale (Mrs. James Haldane), 183, 184, 214, 222-23, *272.
Symmes, John Cleves, 262, *287.

Tappan, Benjamin, 259, *287.
Taylor, ——, of London, 183.
Thomas, ——, of New York, 229.
Thompson, Jeremiah, 229, 234, *281.
Thompson, William, 183, *271-72.
Tiebout, Miss ——, 267.
Tiebout, Cornelius, 266.
Troost, Gerard, 267, 288.
Turner, Sarah, 237, 265, 266, *284.

295

Van Aelst, William, 277.
Van den Bosch, Jan, 196, 204-205, *276.
Vehrli, ——, 195.
Veenhuisen (Vennhuisen), pauper colony in Holland, 200-205.
Velutti, opera singer, 215.
Viardot-García, Pauline, 280.
Visser, ——, 204.
Völker, ——, 182, 183, 184, 215.
Voorsel (Voersel, Belgium), 218.

Wagner, ——, of Canada, 183.
Walker, Mrs. ——, Quaker missionary, 225, 226, 227.
Walker, Charles, 215, *277-78.
Walker, Isaac, 215.
Walker, John, 215, 272, 273, *277, 278.
Ward, Allan, 266.
Wateren, village in Holland, 195.
Wheatley and Adlard, 213, *277.
Wheeler, Mrs. ——, 215.
Wheeling (W. Va.), 242, 244, 245, 259.
Whitwell, Stedman, 185, 256, *274, 288; passenger on "Philanthropist," 257, 266, 268.
Wilkes, Charles, president of the Bank of New York, 230.
Wilmington (Del.), 232.
Wright, Frances, 285, 287.
Wright, J., of Glasgow, 219, *279.

Yellow Springs (Ohio), 245, 286-87.
Yule, Dr. ——, of Edinburgh, 181, 216.

Zeist (Holland), 217.
Zusdyk (?), in Holland, 193.
Zwolle (Holland), 194, 208.

977.2

WESTVILLE N. D. TWP.
PUBLIC LIBRARY

Restricted